AN ENGLISHMAN'S
COMMONPLACE BOOK

ROGER HUDSON is typically English in that one of his grandmothers was from Dublin and the other from New Zealand. His life has been spent with books, publishing them, introducing, editing and compiling them. His longest associations have been with John Murray, the Folio Society, *History Today* and Getty Images. He has also written regularly for *Slightly Foxed* since it began.

AN
ENGLISHMAN'S
COMMONPLACE
BOOK

Roger Hudson

First published by Slightly Foxed in 2020

This collection and introduction © Roger Hudson 2020

Slightly Foxed Ltd
53 Hoxton Square
London N1 6PB

A CIP catalogue record for this book is available from the British Library.

ISBN 978-1-910898-40-6

Printed by Henry Ling Ltd., Dorchester

Introduction

Many of us have bought a notebook, seduced by its proper cloth or leather binding, laid paper and marbled endpapers into thinking we can fill its pages with our equally well-finished thoughts and observations, or keep a diary in it. It is to be our riposte to all those ephemeral electric screens. But after a few pages the entries peter out and we are left with feelings of guilt and some elegantly bound scrap paper.

Nil desperandum. This is when you turn it into a commonplace book instead: no need to cudgel the brain or despair at the banality of your daily life. Start filling the pages with any sentence or passage that particularly strikes you in your reading, confusingly the exact opposite of what's commonplace. But it is not only high-flown extracts from the best literature and the most erudite thinkers or commentators that are allowed. Your newspapers and magazines are as important as sources; then there are conversations, broadcasts, overheard remarks. Variety, the unexpected are what you hope for, a bit of vulgarity and the ridiculous mixed in with the elevated. It must not become at all belle-lettrist, must not read as if it has been chosen by some Edwardian or Georgian 'bookman'. You should find the process of writing down these passages gives you physical pleasure; you might even start using that expensive fountain pen you bought, to indulge in this entirely free pastime, which also meets the urge to collect, so very strong in us.

There are a few rules and some pitfalls to avoid, as well as the belle-lettrist one. It is a good discipline to wait a day or more before putting something you've found into your book, to make sure it stands the test of time, has strength in depth. Too many aphorisms, maxims, epigrams, proverbs, saws, bumper stickers or apothegms are to be avoided, otherwise it becomes like one of those desk calendars where you tear off a page each day to read a new 'thought' on the next. Epitaphs must be outstanding to get included. At the other extreme, avoid passages that are more than a page in length. Ration the amount you allow yourself from Sydney Smith; there are also authors like Patrick Leigh Fermor and Sylvia Townsend Warner who spoil one for choice, so that one gives up on transcribing from their books and instead just scribbles lists of plums on their flyleaves. Do not go on a special search for passages that might make the grade; they must be found in the normal course of your reading. Do not fall back on the endless collections of quotes and sayings to be found only a Google away. In both cases the very process seems to atrophy one's judgement and taste. Do not allow yourself to transfer to your own, passages read in other published commonplace books or anthologies. Number your pages and keep a running index in your book, firstly so that you can find what you want, and secondly as an aid were you to sort and then transcribe your entries.

I have done much sorting and shuffling when selecting from my roughly 40 years' worth of commonplace entries, ending up with 46 headings or subjects. There is little rhyme or reason about the order in which these subjects come and certainly no claim to any sort of comprehensiveness. If I have a particular bias when 'copying out extracts', as our forebears called chrestomathy or the compiling of commonplace books, then it is towards history.

ROGER HUDSON

Contents

Happiness and Pleasure	9
Weather	11
Architecture	14
The Civil War	16
Money	17
France	20
Adlestrop Moments	22
Bigotry and Doubt	25
The Royal Navy	27
Publishing and Books	29
General Sir Charles Napier	31
Food	34
Drink	37
Liberty, Equality, Fraternity	38
Painters	40
Sleep, Stupor, Bliss	41
Sydney Smith	42
Words and Names	44
Love	47
Authors	49
The Gentry	52
Russia	55
Clever, Clever	57
Eternity, the Universe	58
Music and Musicians	59

Contents

Sir Thomas Browne   61

Elizabeth I   62

History   64

Emily Eden   67

Gardens and Parks   70

Opera   73

The First World War   75

The Second World War   77

Politics and Politicians   78

Some Places   82

Royalty   84

The Aristocracy   86

Printing in the Early Days   89

England, Britain   90

Sex   94

Sea and Shore   98

Harriet, Lady Granville   99

Scotland   101

Queen Victoria   102

Death   106

Mixed Motives and Self-Deception   110

Acknowledgements   112

Happiness and Pleasure

Jefferson did not promise happiness, only its pursuit.

Freud said the only true pleasure in life comes from fulfilling in adulthood the desires one wasn't able to satisfy as a child. His was to eat ice cream on the slopes of Vesuvius.

Conceive to yourself 150 to 200 people met together, dressed in the extremity of fashion; painted as red as bacchanals; poisoning the air with perfumes; treading on each other's gowns; making the crowd they blame; not one in ten able to get a chair; protesting they are engaged to ten other places; and lamenting the fatigue they are not obliged to endure; ten or a dozen card-tables, crammed with dowagers of quality, grave ecclesiastics and yellow admirals; and you have an idea of an assembly.

Hannah More the playwright,
soon to turn seriously evangelical, 1782

The true *summum bonum* of human life consists in reading *Tristram Shandy*, or in blowing with a pair of bellows into your shoes in hot weather, and in roasting potatoes in the ashes under the grate in the cold.

Archdeacon William Paley, author of the enormously successful
Evidences of Christianity, 1794, and no evangelical

While Canning [Foreign Secretary] is viewing the scenery of the Lakes, and the King is fishing in a punt on Virginia Water, I am bound to suppose there is no tempest upon the political ocean. I wish that Ferdinand [King of Spain] was hanged – Rothschild, Baring and all the gambling crew in the *Gazette* [i.e. gone bankrupt]

– the Sultan driven forth from Constantinople – his wife and concubines set loose – that balloons were actual and safe conveyances and that I had a villa in the Thracian Bosporus.

Michael Angelo Taylor, a rich Whig MP,
quoted by Thomas Creevey in September 1825

I should like to rise and go
Where the golden apples grow;
Where below another sky
Parrot islands anchored lie,
And, watched by cockatoos and goats,
Lonely Crusoes building boats.

Robert Louis Stevenson,
A Child's Garden of Verses

Marry your children, sack your servants, forget your enemies, remember your friends, enslave your admirers, fatten yourself – and all will yet be well.

Walter Raleigh, first Professor of English at Oxford, *Letters*, 1918

James Agate sets out his ideal way of spending the afternoon and evening when by the sea.
After a keen [golf] match and dinner I listen on the pier or promenade to a band playing Strauss waltzes through which the sea can be faintly heard. The bandstand looks as much as possible like a wedding cake, it is brilliantly lit up, moths flutter, and the smoke of one's cigar goes straight up and is very blue. After the crowd has dispersed one goes to sleep on a bench, until it is one o'clock and it begins to grow cold.

Ego, 1933

Weather

A tremendous gale of wind has acted on me like champagne and cathedral-organs in one.

Charles Kingsley, recuperating in
Ilfracombe, 1849

When I got to the chapel my beard, moustaches and whiskers were so stiff with ice I could hardly open my mouth and my beard was frozen on to my mackintosh . . . the baby was baptized in ice which was broken and swimming about in the font.

The Reverend Francis Kilvert, *Diary*,
Septuagesima Sunday, 1870

A sudden and blessed change in the weather, a south-west wind, pouring warm rain, and the birds in the garden singing like mad creatures, the whole air in a charm and tumult of joy and delight.

Kilvert, *Diary*, March 1875

Weathercock with head where tail ought to be; dark, damp, rotten cutthroat-looking weather; flowers blowing; bluebottles buzzing; doctors galloping in every direction; a philharmonic of blackbirds and thrushes; an armistice from guns and shooting, the poor punters driven to oyster-dredging, eel picking, day labour or beggary.

Colonel Peter Hawker's diary,
Christmas 1843

Punters were the punt-gunners who tried to earn a living shooting wildfowl on the Hampshire coast.

I like de landscapes of Constable . . . but he makes me call for my umbrella and greatcoat.

The Swiss-born painter Henry Fuseli

A raindrop on a windless day falls at 18 m.p.h.

Absolutely pluperfect

Henry Blofeld on *Test Match Special* summing up
the weather during the Lord's Test,
July 2006, a description often used by him

The value of an event on a wet day in the country

Jane Austen, *Mansfield Park*

How fitting that the Prologue to Chaucer's *Canterbury Tales*, the first great piece of English literature, should start with the weather, the sweet showers of April after the drought of March.

Each gust of wind 'made me think of defeated armies, retreating; or of ghosts who were trying desperately to get in for shelter, and then went moaning on'.

Willa Cather, *My Antonia*, of a house on the Nebraska prairie

A cloud comes over Charlotte Street and seems as if it were sailing softly on the April wind to fall in a blessed shower upon the lilac buds and thirsty anemones somewhere in Essex, or, who knows? Perhaps in Boulge [his Suffolk home]. Out will run Mrs Faiers [his housekeeper], and with red arms and face of woe haul in the struggling windows of the cottage, and make all right. Beauty Bob [his parrot] will cast a bird's eye out at the shower, and bless the useful wet. Mr Loder [the Woodbridge stationer] will observe to the farmer for whom he is doing up a dozen of Queen's Heads [the new postage stamps], that it will be a great use; and the farmer will agree that his young barleys wanted it much. The German Ocean [North Sea] will dimple with innumerable pinpoints, and porpoises rolling near the surface sneeze with unusual pellets of fresh water.

Edward Fitzgerald to a Suffolk neighbour from London,

Letters, April 1844

Yesterday had a twang of frost in it.

Sir Walter Scott, *Journal*, 2 May 1826

Architecture

Building certainly ought to have the attribute of eternal, and therefore the only thing incapable of new fashions.

Sir Christopher Wren

A conservatory is certainly the hardest thing to design in a Norman style.

The Victorian architect E. B. Lamb

> In the reigns of Queen Bess and King James
> Few designers are known, and the claims
> That a house is by Smythson
> Are frequently myths, on
> Account of the lack of known names.

Nicholas Cooper on Robert Smythson,
architect of Longleat, Hardwick, etc.

Vanbrugh had to explain to the Duchess of Marlborough what a corridor was, a novelty at the time he was building Blenheim Palace for her.

Ruskin said the new Houses of Parliament were like a magnificent fender.

Style . . . generally has as little relation to the merits of a building as the cut of a man's clothes to the condition of his soul.

H. S. Goodhart-Rendel, *English Architecture since the Regency*, 1953

In 1957 Khrushchev outlawed architectural decoration in the Soviet Union.

A barren phallus of egg boxes, without eggs: the poet Alan Brownjohn's description of the 33-storey Centre Point office block by Tottenham Court Road tube station, completed in 1966 and left empty for many years as its value appreciated. In 1995 it was listed, Grade II. Permission had originally been granted for it in return for the space for a roundabout and traffic scheme at its foot, which never worked and was soon abandoned.

Tower blocks, a permanent combination of lavatory and crime scene

Simon Heffer, *Literary Review*, September 2010

When I complained to its architect Sir Denys Lasdun that no one could find the door to the National Theatre his reply was that 'doors are élitist'. A similar aversion to sloping roofs still baffles me.

Simon Jenkins, reviewing a book on post-war architecture

Massively expensive crazy cottages clad in titanium – Jonathan Meades's description of what he also called sight-bite buildings or logo architecture, the first of which was Frank Gehry's Guggenheim Museum, 1997, in Bilbao

The Civil War

We are running headlong to destruction and, like butchers, one to quarter out the other: brother against brother, father against son, friend against friend, and all for I know not what. Religion to be purified is the pretence of some, liberty to be preserved is the profession of others.

Edward Sackville, 4th Earl of Dorset

He wrote this in August 1642, as the war was beginning. His younger son was to be murdered by Parliamentary soldiers in 1645 after being captured. There is a painting of a beautiful young man, eyes closed, lying dead in bed, only his head to be seen above the covers, by an unknown hand in the National Portrait Gallery. It is thought to be him.

Sir Jacob Astley, commander of the Cavalier foot at Edgehill, the first battle of the war in October 1642, is remembered today for his prayer before it commenced: 'O Lord, Thou knowest how busy I must be this day: if I forget Thee, do not Thou forget me.' He should also be remembered for his prophetic remark to his captors in March 1646 after the raw Welsh levies under his command put up little fight before laying down their arms at Stow-on-the-Wold, in the last action of the war: 'You have done your work, boys. You may go play, unless you fall out among yourselves.'

Harry, Lord Bellamont, the Cavalier, said on his capture in 1646, 'that he had taken up arms neither for religion, for there were then so many he knew not which to be of, nor for that mousetrap, the laws, but to re-establish the King on his throne; and seeing therefore the time had not yet come, he desired leave that they would discharge him.'

Money

The value of money has been settled by general consent to express our wants and our property, as letters were invented to express our ideas; and both these institutions, by giving more active energy to the powers and passions of human nature, have contributed to multiply the objects they were designed to represent.

Edward Gibbon

The historian G. M. Young said that if asked 'What is prose?' this would have been the first sentence to come into his mind.

All the world loves the Swiss franc, but only the Swiss love the centime.

You must never confuse genius with a bull market.

A nineteenth-century Rothschild replied, when asked the secret of his success: 'Always selling too soon.'

Turnover is vanity, profit is sanity.

John, Lord Sainsbury

Profit is an accountant's opinion, but cash is a fact.

Terry Smith, *Accounting for Growth*

The saying *Pecunia non olet* – money does not smell – was attributed to the Emperor Vespasian when he put a tax on the urine collected from Rome's public lavatories. It was used by tanners and for the cleaning of woollen garments. Joan Rivers, the comedienne, had a variant on this: 'Money makes a good deodorant.'

Coper was a dashing [horse] dealer, always rounding his figures and going for guineas [rather than pounds].

Robert Surtees, *Mr Facey Romford's Hounds*, 1864

As long as the music is playing, you've got to get up and dance. We're still dancing.

Chuck Prince of Citibank, July 2007, just before the crash

It is the highest impertinence and presumption in kings and ministers to pretend to watch over the economy of private people, and to restrain their expense. They are themselves, always, and without exception, the greatest spendthrifts in the society.

Adam Smith, *The Wealth of Nations*, 1776

J. M. Keynes was responsible for the investments of his college, King's, Cambridge. He ended by doubling its income but in 1936, speculating in the commodities market, he was about to be forced to take delivery of a month's supply of wheat for Britain from Argentina and seriously planned to store it in King's Chapel, until told the building was too small. So, playing for time, he raised objections to the wheat's quality. It took a month to clean it, during which the price rose sufficiently to allow him to sell it without loss.

We are indebted for all the noblest exertions of human genius, for everything that distinguishes the civilised from the savage state . . . [to] the laws of property and marriage, and to the apparently narrow principle of self-interest which prompts each individual to exert himself in bettering his condition.

The Revered Thomas Malthus (1766–1834), pioneering economist

Inherited wealth and the recycling effect: first in bare statistics, then poetically in some lines from the 'Epistle to Bathurst' by Alexander Pope

Only 15 per cent of families that become wealthy manage to stay that way beyond three generations. In 20 per cent of cases the wealth is dissipated much quicker.

> Riches, like insects, when conceal'd they lie,
> Wait but for wings, and in their season, fly.
> Who sees pale Mammon pine amidst his store,
> Sees but a backward steward for the poor;
> This year a reservoir, to keep and spare,
> The next a fountain, spouting through his heir,
> In lavish streams to quench a Country's thirst,
> And men and dogs shall drink him 'till they burst.

Mansa Musa I, ruler of Mali in the fourteenth century, had a net worth of $400 billion in today's money. He is reckoned by some to be the richest man of all time. Alan Rufus, Count of Brittany and Lord of Richmond, North Yorkshire, was worth the equivalent of $179 billion at his death in 1093, making him the richest Briton.

The economic liberal deal: you get to offer in the first act a betterment to customers, but you don't get to arrange for protection later from competitors. After making your bundle in the first act, you suffer from competition in the second. Too bad. By the end of the third act, after those pesky imitators have entered in the second, everyone's rich.

Economist and historian Deirdre McCloskey,
author of the *Bourgeois Era* trilogy, 2006–16

France

The French: understandably the most self-centred of people
Kenneth Clark in his essay 'An Art Historian's Apology'

Kenneth Clark stands in front of Notre-Dame in Paris in the first episode of the *Civilisation* television series and says, 'What is Civilisation? I don't know. I can't define it. But I think I can recognise it when I see it, and in fact I'm looking at it now.' It was May 1968, the time of 'Les Evénements', when this was being filmed and what was actually in sight were protesting students about to be charged by riot police. Clark and the director Michael Gill were soon choking on tear gas.

'*Je suis Marxiste, tendance Groucho.*'
A 1968 student placard

Woody Allen's character in *Deconstructing Harry*, accused of being no more than an admixture of sarcasm and orgasm, said that in France he would have run, and won, on that ticket.

They are like children, clever, lively, troublesome children . . . If kept in order, gay and animated, easily pleased and rarely offended. I do not think them as a nation false or capricious, or that they are to be measured by the same rule as other people on earth. Their impressions are all uncommonly vivid. Their expressions of affection, admiration, delight proportionately strong. You deceive yourself if you reckon upon this, but it is your own fault.
Harriet, Lady Granville, wife of the new Ambassador to France, in 1824
How she found the French upper classes whom she had to deal with and entertain

Lizelotte, Princess Palatine and wife of the Duc d'Orléans, younger brother of Louis XIV, whom she admired, dismissed his bastard children by his mistress, Madame de Montespan, as 'mouse droppings amongst the pepper'.

Simon Winder in his book *Germania* remarks on 'the sheer absurdity of Louis XIV's court, with everyone watching the King shitting or admiring his ballet moves (dressed as sunshine)'.

The Countess of Bessborough reported a conversation she had in 1803 in Paris during the short Peace of Amiens with the French General Moreau, who had become increasingly hostile to Napoleon since his seizure of power in 1799: 'He never forgets that he is Corsican and that Corsica has been enslaved by France, and I can assure you that there is nothing he detests more in the world than the French, with the sole exception of your nation.'

The future Emperor Louis-Napoleon after his election as President in 1848: 'I am prepared to be baptised with the waters of universal suffrage, but I do not intend to live with my feet in a puddle.'

Georges Clemenceau, Prime Minister, for the second time, from 1917 to 1920: '*Si je pouvois pisser comme Lloyd George parle!*' And then on President Woodrow Wilson: '*Il parle comme Jesus-Christ, mais il se conduit comme Lloyd George.*'

In 1966, when President de Gaulle demanded the removal of US forces from France as a consequence of the French withdrawal from NATO, President Johnson asked whether that included the dead ones. On a state visit to Britain de Gaulle was entertained to dinner by the Queen in the Waterloo Chamber at Windsor Castle, its walls hung with pictures of the leaders of Britain's allies from 150 or more years before. De Gaulle gestured towards them and asked: '*Alors, pour battre Napoléon il vous a fallu tous ces messieurs?*'

Adlestrop Moments

Edward Thomas's poem is far too well known to include in full, but here is the first verse as a reminder:

> Yes, I remember Adlestrop –
> The name, because one afternoon
> Of heat the express-train drew up there
> Unwontedly. It was late June.

Others have encountered similar suspended moments.

Clarbeston Road – 9 a.m. A boy walks slowly down the length of the platform touching the cardboard boxes warming in the morning sun, flicking the string of a parcel, looking down the wide empty rail and waiting for the train to Fishguard, which is puffing quietly and blowing out steam further down the line and getting ready to come in – rather like an elderly actress once famous who knows her best days are over and that it is only a small country theatre half full but determined all the same to do her best. Ugly and uncomfortable, there is a sense of security about railway stations which the luxury and comfort of an airport lounge can never provide.

Keith Vaughan, Journal, 5 June 1962

> When the Circle train was held up by a signal
> Between Gloucester Road and High Street (Ken)
> In the battering dog-day heat of August
> We sweated and mopped our brows. And then
> We saw in the cutting, amid the loosestrife
> And butterflies looping through bindweed trails,
> A boy who lay drinking, straight from the bottle,
> When of course, he was paid to look at the rails.

The first verse of 'Incident in August' by Brian Morgan

The Circle Line trains nearly always seem to stop there, giving priority to District Line ones going to and from Earls Court. I have seen foxes while waiting, but no boy swigging from a bottle.

It was the very point of perfection in the heart of an English May-day. The unseen tides of air had turned, and all nature was setting its face with the shadows of the horse-chestnuts towards the peace of the coming night . . . What a Garden of Eden it was, this fatted, clipped and washen land! . . . A light puff of wind – it scattered flakes of may over the gleaming rails – gave me a faint whiff as it might have been of fresh coconut, and I knew that the golden gorse was in bloom somewhere out of sight. Linnaeus had thanked God on his bended knee when he first saw a field of it.

Rudyard Kipling, 'My Sunday at Home', from *The Day's Work*

It was a pleasant journey though; the train was a huge one, and it seemed to be just abandoned at stations by all concerned – stood idly waiting until it occurred to some official to try if he could start it.

A. C. Benson, *Diary*, 1911

The Regular Magistrate, Major Sinclair Yeates, is going on what seems like an interminable and complicated train journey to a family wedding somewhere the other end of Ireland; his luggage includes a large salmon wrapped in disintegrating newspaper, intended as part of the wedding breakfast. At this point in the story, the railway is a single line.

I awoke in total darkness; the train was motionless, and complete and profound silence reigned. We were at a station, that much I discerned by the light of a dim lamp at the far end of the platform glistening with wet. I struck a match and ascertained it was eleven o'clock, precisely the hour at which I was to board the mail train. I jumped out and ran down the platform; there was no one in the train; there was no one even on the engine, which was forlornly hissing to itself in silence. There was not a human being anywhere. Every door was closed, and all was dark. The name-board of the station was faintly visible; with a lighted match I went along it letter by letter. It seemed as if the whole alphabet were in it, and by the time I had got to the end I had forgotten the beginning. One fact I had, however, mastered, that it was not the junction at which I was to catch the mail. [Then he saw a chink of light under a door.] A voice was suddenly uplifted within. 'Your best now agin that. Throw down your Jack!' I opened the door with pardonable violence, and found the guard, the stationmaster, the driver, and the stoker, seated on barrels round a packing case, on which they were playing a game of cards . . . I accepted the statements that they thought there wasn't a Christian in the train, that a few minutes here or there wouldn't signify, that they would have me at the junction in twenty minutes, and it was often the mail was late . . . 'Mind the goods, Tim!' shouted the stationmaster, as he slammed my door, 'She might be coming any time now!'

The answer travelled magnificently back from the engine.

'Let her come! She'll meet her match!' A war-whoop upon the steam whistle fittingly closed the speech, and the train sprang into action.

E. OE. Somerville and Martin Ross, 'Poisson d'Avril',
from *Further Experiences of an Irish R. M.*, 1908

Bigotry and Doubt

Protestants and Catholics united in their hatred of ecumenicism

Ulster newspaper headline

Said the Frenchwoman sitting next to Charles Moore: 'We are not anti-Semitic. It is all lies. The newspapers only say this because they are controlled by Jews.'

The terrible simplifiers

Jacob Burckhart, 1889

And if I revelled in your melancholy
(Like mooching through the rain without a brolly)
It was the passion of your doubt I loved,
Your castigation of the bigot's folly.

From 'Letter to Omar' by Dick Davis

It is Omar Khayyám whom he addresses. He is Professor Emeritus of Persian at Ohio State University.

To go from being a Brownie to a Girl Guide you had to pass in General Information, Knitting and Rice Pudding. [When she saw hers come out of the oven, almost raw] I braced myself for failure but not for being called, as I was, a disgrace to the ideals of Baden-Powell.

The novelist Penelope Fitzgerald, *A House of Air: Selected Writings*

I am a man of no convictions, or at least I think I am.

A line from *The Philanthropist* (1970) by Christopher Hampton

Tom Stoppard called this his favourite line in modern drama.

Is it therefore infallibly agreeable to the word of God, all that you say? I beseech you in the bowels of Christ, think it possible you may be mistaken . . . Bethink yourselves; we hope you do.

Oliver Cromwell addressing the
Scottish Presbyterians, August 1650

Dubius, sed non improbus vixi. Incertus morior non perturbatus; Humanum est Nescire et Errare. Deo Confido Omnipotenti Benevolentissimo. Ens Entium Miserere mei.

I have lived doubtful but dutiful. I die uncertain but unperturbed; it is human to be ignorant and to err. I trust in the all-powerful and most benevolent God. May the Supreme Being have mercy on me.

The epitaph on the monument in Henry VII's Chapel in Westminster
Abbey to John Sheffield, 1st Duke of Buckingham of the second
creation (1648–1721), friend and patron of Dryden and Pope

A mourning figure of his third wife, an illegitimate daughter of James II, sits on the monument. In the 1680s he had been banned from Court for flirting with her legitimate half-sister, the future Queen Anne. Samantha Cameron, née Sheffield, is descended from the Duke's illegitimate son.

The man who was consumed by conspiracy theories until, one day, he announced that he no longer believed in any of them since they were all concocted by the government

The Royal Navy

I recollect from infancy seeing French frigates sailing into Portsmouth harbour, dismasted, and running along the seashore, cheering till my throat was parched.

The painter Benjamin Robert Haydon, 1813

Sir Adam Ferguson, a prisoner-of-war there after his capture in the Peninsular War, described the arrival at Verdun of 'a regiment which the French had formed partly of deserters from various nations, among them some English. In the street were some English sailors of the Nelson breed, prisoners, men with long pigtails. The deportment of these, upon the deserters endeavouring to claim kindred and acquaintance: no abuse or answer, but a silent and almost compassionate discharge of tobacco juice.'

Lord Ellesmere, Personal Reminiscences of the
Duke of Wellington

The marshbird squeal of boatswains' whistles

My Foreign Country: Trevor Fishlock's Britain, 1997

WANTED: Stout able-bodied men who can run a mile without stopping with a sackful of Spanish dollars on their backs

Lord Cochrane's advertisement for extra crew for his ship,
the Impérieuse, 1806

Submariners are regarded by the rest of the Navy as 'a sort of dirty habit in tins'.

Admiral Sir Sandy Woodward,
himself a submariner

Of the British forces in Corsica in 1794, the viceroy there, Lord Minto, said the Naval officers were full of energy and action, while with the Army officers, 'it is all high lounge and still life'.

The names of the gunboats under Nelson in the English Channel in 1801:
Cracker, Boxer, Flamer, Haughty, Attack, Plumper, Bruiser, Wolfe, Griper, Conflict, Archer, Vixen, Minx, Bold, Locust, Jackal, Constant, Monkey, Mariner, Mallard, Snipe, Charger, Ferreter

The table at which Kaiser Wilhelm II signed the documents for the mobilization of the German army and navy on 1 August 1914 was made from oak taken from HMS *Victory* and the stand for stationery on it was a model of the ship complete with the flags of Nelson's famous signal. After the Japanese Admiral Togo had defeated the Russian fleet at the Battle of Tsushima in 1905, he waited to return to port until 21 October, the hundredth anniversary of Trafalgar. He had attended the Royal Naval College at Dartmouth, and thought he was literally a reincarnation of Nelson.

In the 1950s a US flagship sailed into Hong Kong and signalled to the British port admiral: 'Good morning, how is the second-largest navy in the world?' The reply was, 'We're fine. How is the second-best?'

Publishing and Books

Pope made the equivalent of over a million dollars from his translation of the *Iliad* (1715–20). Richard Bentley, the classical scholar and despotic Master of Trinity College, Cambridge, said to Pope that it was 'a very pretty poem, but you must not call it the *Iliad*'.

Darwin's *On the Origin of Species* (1859) only sold about 7,000 copies in the first five years after publication.

R. D. Blackmore's novel *Lorna Doone* (1869) was easily the best-selling of all the 950 titles published under the old Everyman's Library imprint.

A great book is often ahead of its time, and the trick is how to keep it afloat until the times catch up with it.

The American publisher Robert Giroux

All the runaway bestsellers galloping into oblivion

The American novelist Peter de Vries

So impossible to guess what that great ass, the public, is going to take to its vague and shapeless bosom

George Lyttelton writing to the publisher Rupert Hart-Davis

The publisher J. M. Dent was a very emotional man. One day I went into his office when he was signing royalty cheques and the tears were running down his cheeks.

The author Frank Swinnerton

A rogue, of course, but a civil one
>> Jane Austen's opinion of her publisher, John Murray II

[The publishers] George Macmillan and John Murray [IV] are playing billiards downstairs, *not together*. Dog does not eat dog.
>> Walter Raleigh, writing from the Athenaeum, 1909

The woman going into a bookshop and asking for a copy of *Tess of the Dormobiles*

When St Augustine caught St Ambrose reading silently, he was awestruck.

In 1992 it was calculated that more books had been published in the previous five years than in the entire history of publishing.

Les Hauts de Hurlevent – the French title of *Wuthering Heights*

The sense – essential to mature enjoyment of any classic – of being entirely free from responsibility to pause for a second over anything that threatens the least sign of tedium
>> Nicholas Jenkins, the narrator in Anthony Powell's twelve-volume novel sequence, *A Dance to the Music of Time*, while reading Harington's translation of *Orlando Furioso* (1591), in the last volume of the sequence (1975)

The laudable practice of skipping
>> Sir Walter Scott

General Sir Charles Napier

Napier (1782–1853) was not a 'Sepoy General' who had spent his life in India, but a veteran of the Peninsular War, from which he emerged with seven wounds. He had then become the Resident of Cephalonia when the Ionian Islands came under British control for a few decades, and in 1839 had been given command of the northern district of England at a time of great labour unrest. He gained much praise for his handling of a volatile situation and then in 1842, what Emily Eden so shrewdly identified as 'one of those pretences for interference England delights in' arose in Sind, part of present-day Pakistan to the west and east of the Indus. Aged over 60, he was given command of the force sent to tame the Amirs there, as corrupt, ruthless and despotic a set of rulers as could be found in Asia. These days, he is remembered, if at all, because of his statue with its enormous beaky nose in Trafalgar Square, and as one of the remarkable sons of Lady Sarah Lennox, the subject, with her three sisters, of Stella Tillyard's 1995 bestseller Aristocrats. *That this is so, is quite wrong.*

In February 1843, with 800 British and 1,400 Indian troops, he defeated the Amirs' army ten times that size at Meeanee. Nearly every European officer was killed but Napier somehow survived.

I was obliged to ride between the fires of two lines not twenty yards apart. I expected death as much from our men as from the enemy, and I was much singed by our fire; my whiskers twice or thrice so, and my face peppered by fellows who, in their fear, fired high over all heads but mine, and nearly scattered my brains. [In March there was a second battle with the same ridiculous odds and same result, at Dubba.] The Baluchis are most determined fatalists, and most terrible swordsmen: they cut through everything. Heads fly off at a blow! It has been repeatedly done, and it is the same with an arm . . . No Baluchi assailed me personally, though several came near, and one I covered but did not shoot, having great repugnance to kill with my own hand unless attacked . . . [My men] were like cucumbers.

Napier called the campaign 'a very advantageous, useful, humane piece of rascality'. He then matched his peacekeeping to his understanding of the locals. A chief asked for pardon for a retainer who was sentenced for wife-murder.

'No! I will hang him!'

'What! You will hang a man for only killing his wife?'

'Yes; she had done no wrong.'

'Wrong, no. But he was angry, why should he not kill her?'

'Well, I am angry, why should I not kill him?'

When priests argued that the sacred and ancient custom of wife-burning, suttee, should be respected, Napier replied:

'Be it so. This burning of widows is your custom; prepare the funeral pile. But my nation has also a custom. When men burn women alive we hang them, and confiscate all their property. My carpenters shall therefore erect gibbets on which to hang all concerned when the widow is consumed. Let us all act according to national customs.'

In 1847 he allowed himself to dream a little.

Were I emperor of the East and thirty years of age I would have Constantinople on one side and Pekin on the other before twenty years, and all between should be grand, free and happy. The Emperor of Russia should be *done*: freedom and the press should burn along his frontier like touch-paper, until half his subjects were mine in heart; and then I would smite him under the fifth rib, and the Baltic should be my north-west province. Odin went from India to Scandinavia, so would I, and crack the ice under his throne at St Petersburg. What stuff is all this! Here am I, sixty-six years old and in bodily pain, fit for nothing but the grave.

He was entirely clearsighted in his view that Britain held India by force, but his long-term hopes for it were wonderfully liberal for his time. If only more had shared his outlook the Indian Mutiny might not have followed a few years later.

Seize every point of strength by arms, keep them by arms, and show ourselves resolved to rule the Empire we have won. It is true we have won that Empire most unjustly, but it is now impossible to abandon our position. We may not retreat, and can only hold our ground by skill and courage. It is not by moderation but by victory that we must hold India; and we must mix with the people, give them justice, give them riches, give them honours, give them share of all things, until we blend with them and become one nation. When a half-caste, or a full native, can be Governor-General, we shall not hold India as a colony or conquest, but be part-inhabitants, and as numerous as will be required to hold it as our own.

Extracts from *The Life and Opinions of General Sir Charles James Napier* by W. F. P. Napier, 4 vols, 1857

Food

Cooking enabled hominids to trade gut size for brain size.

        Matthew Ridley, *The Rational Optimist*, 2010

An al fresco lunch of hock and wasps

        James Agate, *Ego*, July 1937

> The man had sure a palate cover'd o'er
> With brass or steel, that on the rocky shore
> First broke the oozy oyster's pearly coat,
> And risqu'd the living morsel down his throat.
> What will not luxury taste? Earth, sea and air
> Are daily ransack'd for the bill of fare.
> Blood stuff'd in skins is British christians' food,
> And France robs marshes of the croaking brood;
> Spongy morells in strong ragousts are found,
> And in the soupe the slimy snail is drown'd.

        John Gay, *Trivia or the Art of Walking the Streets of London*, 1716

In the Anglo-Indian vocabulary scrambled eggs were known as rumble-tumble; in Spain they are *huevos revueltos*.

Kippers as big as wicket-keepers' gloves

        My Foreign Country: Trevor Fishlock's Britain

Green bursting figs, and tunnies steeped in brine

        Matthew Arnold, 'The Scholar Gypsy'

If bees produce honey, why don't earwigs produce chutney?

        Eddie Izzard

Lord Delamere was a leading figure among the pioneer settlers in Kenya, and there his invariable supper was gazelle chops, blanc-mange, tinned peaches and 'All Aboard for Margate' on the gramophone.

In 1945 an ADC to the Governor of Bengal went into the kitchens to find the servant responsible for making toast lying on the floor with his bare feet directed at the open door of the stove and slices of bread between his toes.

> . . . lasagne so tempting to swallow
> In slippery ropes,
> And gourds fried in great purple slices,
> That colour of popes.
> Meantime, see the grape bunch they've brought you:
> The rain-water slips
> O'er the heavy blue bloom on each globe
> Which the wasp to your lips
> Still follows with fretful persistence:
> Nay, taste, while awake,
> This half of a curd-white smooth cheese-ball
> That peels, flake by flake,
> Like an onion, each smoother and whiter;
> Next sip this weak wine
> From the thin green glass flask, with its stopper,
> A leaf of the vine:
> And end with the prickly-pear's red flesh
> That leaves through its juice
> The stony black seeds on your pearl-teeth.
> Sirocco is loose!
>
> Robert Browning, 'The Englishman in Italy'

The lasagne sounds like tagliatelle and the gourd like aubergine.

Battered codpieces. Seen on an English menu in Mytilene in the 1960s by the classical scholar, Peter Green

Charles Lamb's definition of quintessence: an apple pie made all of quinces

In the eighteenth century, pineapples could be hired by the day to impress your guests. It has been calculated that it cost £569 to produce one in 1868, and as late as the 1920s, the grandest dinner parties had both 'a pineapple and Lady Curzon'.

'Presiding over an establishment like this makes sad havoc with the features, my dear Miss Pecksniffs,' said Mrs Todgers. 'The gravy alone, is enough to add twenty years to one's age, I do assure you.'

'Lor!' cried the two Miss Pecksniffs.

'The anxiety of that one item, my dears, keeps the mind continually upon the stretch. There is no passion in human nature, as the passion for gravy among commercial gentlemen.'

Dickens, *Martin Chuzzlewit*
Mrs Todgers kept a 'boarding house for young gentlemen'.

Slow Food: a triumph of PR on behalf of root vegetables grown on the moral high ground

Jonathan Meades, in a speech at the
Royal Academy summer dinner, 2017

Drink

I assure you, Madame, I can drink safely – I am so close to the ground already.

Henri de Toulouse-Lautrec

Lapsang Souchong, the Islay malt whisky of China teas, or vice versa

A wine merchant described his House White as having '*idées au dessus de sa gare*'.

Red wine goes with meat but white wine goes with carpets.

Katharine Whitehorn, *Cooking in a Bedsitter*

Galsworthy's character James Forsyte was gloomy about the fate of his claret after his death since it 'would be spoilt or drunk, he shouldn't wonder'.

Don't drink and drive, don't even putt.

Dean Martin

If your bloodstream's unwilling to flow
And your heartbeat ticks slow, quick quick, slow,
Let corpuscles cavort,
Circulate Taylor's Port
And soon you'll have all systems go.

Many years ago Taylors used to run a yearly competition for verses about their port – the prize for any published was a dozen bottles. This effort by me made it into print, the first time any of my verse has, and probably the last.

Liberty, Equality, Fraternity

Sois mon frère, ou je te tue.
What the aphorist Nicolas Chamfort said Liberty, Equality, Fraternity would come to in the end. He had been secretary to Louis XVI's sister, popular at Court for his wit, but was then an enthusiastic republican, among the first to enter the Bastille. This was not enough to prevent him from being arrested in 1793 for his remark. He tried to take his own life, shooting himself in the eye and slashing his throat, but finally succumbed to pneumonia.

The great object is to prevent democracy from destroying liberty. In particular, it is to prevent it from destroying economic liberty, a necessary condition of prosperity, but one which leads to a large measure of inequality, envy and division.

> Jonathan, Lord Sumption, historian of the Hundred
> Years War and former Justice of the Supreme Court

If inequality is seen as automatically evil, then socialism will always seem like the better answer. This was a key perception of Margaret Thatcher . . . She publicly identified equality as the enemy of human fulfilment.

> Charles Moore, *The Spectator*, 2006

It is better to cherish virtue and humanity, by leaving much to free will, even with some loss to the object, than to attempt to make men mere machines and instruments of a political benevolence. The world on the whole will gain by a liberty, without which virtue cannot exist.

> Edmund Burke, *Reflections on the Revolution in France*, 1790

Perfect equality means that human liberties must be restrained so that the ablest and most gifted are not permitted to advance beyond those who would inevitably lose if there were competition.

Security, and indeed freedoms, cannot be preserved if freedom to subvert them is permitted.

Justice . . . is not fully compatible with mercy.

[C]ompromises, trade-offs, arrangements have to be made if the worst is not to happen . . . you must believe me, one cannot have everything one wants.

[I]n the end the passionate idealists forget the omelette and just go on breaking eggs.

> Points from the 'Credo' sent by Isaiah Berlin to
> Toronto University, when awarded an honorary doctorate in 1994,
> *Affirming: Letters 1975–1997*

Universal principles . . . necessarily presuppose uniform and perfect subjects, which are to be found in the ideas of pure geometry and (I trust) in the realities of Heaven, but never, never in creatures of flesh and blood.

> Coleridge on the radical political ideas of Major John
> Cartwright, advocate of parliamentary reform

Painters

The nipple should always be a little above the centre. In Rubens and common nature it is below, which gives a flabby, infirm look.

Benjamin Robert Haydon, January 1825

In front of Hals's paintings one longs to paint; in front of Rembrandt's one wants to give up.

The German artist Max Liebermann

Turner's pictures are representations not properly of the objects of nature as of the medium through which they are seen . . . They are pictures of the elements of air, earth and water.

William Hazlitt

The sky is the chief organ of sentiment.

John Constable

Millais once confessed that the only thing he enjoyed about portrait-painting was putting the highlights on the boots of his subjects; the only thing I really enjoy about writing is the punctuation.

James Agate

Sargent often found his female sitters so vacuous and tiresome that he had to retire behind a screen and put out his tongue at them.

When an accountant advised Francis Bacon to live in Switzerland he answered, 'What a terrible prospect. All those fucking views!'

Andy Warhol is an artist as Fergie is a royal.

The novelist Julian Barnes

Sleep, Stupor, Bliss

Sleep takes off the costume of circumstance and arms us with terrible freedom, so that every will rushes to a deed.

Ralph Waldo Emerson

The heavy raindrops struck him with a thousand tingling little thrills, and the weight of all time since time was made hung heavy on his eyelids.

The effect of opium, from Rudyard Kipling's short story, 'The Bridge-Builders', in *The Day's Work*

Carlyle spoke of once having fainted: 'Torrents of sleep descended on the brain; death, I have thought, will be like that.'

William Allingham, *Diary*

After taking opium one feels as if one's soul is being rubbed down with silk.

Henry Bulwer to Richard Monckton Milnes

Save me from curious Conscience, that still holds
Its strength for darkness, burrowing like a mole;
Turn the key deftly in the oiled wards,
And seal the hushed casket of my soul.

The last four lines of John Keats's sonnet on sleep

The winds come to me from the fields of sleep.

William Wordsworth, 'Intimations of Immortality'

Sydney Smith

'The Smith of Smiths', as Macaulay labelled him (1771–1845), was a clergyman and also, as one of the wittiest men of his or any age, a regular ornament at the dinners and entertainments of Whig high society. Early in his career he had been one of the founders of the Edinburgh Review *and his social criticism and comments on contemporary morality continued to appear there for many years. He also regularly mocked many aspects of the Church of England.*

In a review of Charles Waterton's Wanderings in South America, *1826:*
The sloth moves suspended, rests suspended, sleeps suspended, and passes his life in suspense – like a young clergyman distantly related to a bishop . . . The bird whose cry is more powerful than the belfry of a cathedral, ringing for a new dean – just appointed on account of shabby politics, small understanding, and good family.

To Lord Melbourne, à propos his continual swearing:
Let us assume everybody and everything to be damned and come to the point.

On Bishop Henry Phillpotts, inflexible doyen of the old High Church party:
I must believe in the Apostolic Succession. How else can I account for the direct line of descent from Judas Iscariot to the Bishop of Exeter?

He answers two invitations from the domineering Whig hostess, Lady Holland, the first in 1811, the second in 1842:

How very odd, dear Lady Holland, to ask me to dine with you on Sunday the 9th, when I am coming to stay with you from the 5th to the 12th! It is like giving a gentleman an assignation for Wednesday, when you are going to marry him on the preceding Sunday – an attempt to combine the stimulus of gallantry with the security of connubial relations.

I have not the heart, when an amiable lady says, 'Come to *Semiramis* in my box', to decline; but I get bolder at a distance. *Semiramis* would be to me pure misery. I love music very little – hate acting; I have the worst opinion of Semiramis herself, and the whole thing (I cannot help it) seems so childish and so foolish that I cannot abide it. Moreover, it would be rather out of etiquette for a Canon of St Paul's to go to an opera; and where etiquette prevents me from doing things disagreeable to myself, I am a perfect martinet.

To his son-in-law, Dr Henry Holland, 1835:
I am suffering from my old complaint, the hay-fever (as it is called). My fear is of perishing by deliquescence. I melt away in nasal and lachrymal profluvia . . . The [nostrils'] membrane is so irritable that light, dust, contradiction, an absurd remark, the sight of a dissenter – anything sets me a-sneezing and if I begin to sneeze at twelve I don't leave off until two o'clock – and am heard distinctly in Taunton, when the wind sets that way, at a distance of six miles. Turn your mind to this little curse. If consumption is too powerful for physicians at least they should not suffer themselves to be outwitted by such little upstart disorders as the hay-fever.

To Bishop Blomfield:
You must not think me necessarily foolish because I am facetious, nor will I consider you necessarily wise because you are grave.

Words and Names

Artless Pitts, Mince Bubb, Nathannerooe and Truthold and Sekh-
faith Wood, Flourice Cowp, Darsun Fitcher, Humphrey Crumpt
Names from the Tewkesbury Abbey archives

Obscene: the use of this word in a non-sexual context is an infallible
mark of the Left.
Paul Johnson on the late Bishop Jenkins of Durham

Beware the word *social.* When it is used as an adjective it will re-
verse or negate the meaning of the noun to which it is applied:
social contract, social market economy, social conscience, social
democrat, social worker.
Enoch Powell
Social justice and social purpose would now have to be added.

Tzintzuntzan means hummingbird in Purepecham, a Mexican
dialect.
A wisp of snipe – the best collective noun
Bubbly Mary: pidgin for an expectant woman
There is a Japanese word which means, 'Try out a new sword on a
chance passer-by.'

Yeats, when diagnosed with a heart condition that was probably
going to kill him, said he'd rather be called an Advanced Cardio-
Scelerotic than Lord of Lower Egypt.

I'd sooner have a full bottle in front of me than a full frontal
lobotomy.

The Honourable Thomas Kenyon, Filazer, Exigenter and Clerk of Outlawries to the Court of King's Bench, was receiving £1,254 a year from these sinecures until they were finally abolished in 1826. George Selwyn was Surveyor of the Meltings and Clerk of the Irons at the Mint. These sinecures passed to Spencer Perceval, the future prime minister, in 1790. Horace Walpole (d. 1797) was Usher to the Exchequer, Clerk of the Estreats and Comptroller of the Pipe.

Some 'Buddh' words, from the private vocabulary used by the Anglo-Irish Somerville and Ross families, and their relations:
Allegator: someone of malicious tongue; Bosom-salad: corsage; Doldrumizing: inertia; Flahoola: a large, loud woman; Hightum: Sunday frock; Jinks and Snobs: an ill-carved helping of meat; Pollywog: insect; Spitalloo: excessively polite note; Wiley-beguiley: artful.

The Turkish word for asparagus is *kush-konmaz*, literally 'that upon which no bird can sit'. *Imam Bayildi*, a dish of stuffed aubergine, means, 'the priest fainted with delight'.

Percy Crush, footman, Sarah Death, housemaid and Shotbolt the butler: servants at Thrumpton Hall, Nottinghamshire, in the 1920s
Miranda Seymour, *In My Father's House*, 2008

According to *Kelly's Directory*, in 1937 the principal landowners in Beccles, Norfolk, were Messrs Walter Whalebelly and Frederick Teat.

In 1866 the Reverend Benjamin Armstrong, vicar of East Dereham, 'married a young parishioner of the name of Mahershallalashbaz Tuck. His father wished to call him by the shortest name in the Bible, Uz. But the clergyman making some demur, the father said in pique, "Well, if he cannot have the shortest he shall have the longest."'

A Norfolk Diary

The Reverend Ralph William Lyonel Tollemache (1826–96), rector of South Witham, Lincolnshire, a member of the family of the Earls of Dysart, christened his children to excess, but there was no one to stop him. For example, there was: Lyulph Ydwallo Odin Nestor Egbert Lyonel Foedmag Hugh Erchenwyne Saxon Esa Cromwell Orma Nevill Dysart Plantagenet (b. 1876) and Lyonella Fredegunda Cuthberga Ethelswytha Ideh Ysabel Grace Monica de Orellana Plantagenet (b. 1882)

Some Norfolk usages: Bishy-barney-bee: ladybird; Tittermorter: see-saw; Trickalating: decorating; Slant-and-dicular: out of true; Cum on in out onnit: come in out of the rain; The best part of sumtyme: when a job might be finished

The seven bells of Croyland Abbey: Bega, Pega, Turketyl, Tatwin, Beltyn, Bartholomew and Guthlac. Three of the Exeter Cathedral bells: Chanterel (little singer), Salterel (dancer) and Clerematyn (clear morning)

Love

In Naples in 1792 Lord Bruce fell desperately in love with the Duchesse de Fleury – 'like a rabbit with a bunch of parsley', according to Lady Malmesbury.

I can neither eat nor sleep for thinking of you my dearest love. I never touch even pudding you know the reason.

Nelson to Emma Hamilton

Children are time made flesh. To love a child is to love a cloud; a child changes, slips through our fingers, disappears, probably physically but anyway into the adult. It is a love with no end in view save separation, it has no consummation, is nothing except what it is and every day is a fresh blow of the wedge.

P. J. Kavanagh, *People and Places*

The cure of unconquerable passions, and the transfer of unchanging attachments, must vary as to time in different people.

Jane Austen, *Mansfield Park*

This refers to Edmund Bertram's transfer of his affections from Mary Crawford to Fanny Price.

Mr Casaubon kept his hands behind him and allowed her pliant arm to cling with difficulty against his rigid arm. There was something horrible to Dorothea in the sensation which this unresponsive hardness inflicted on her. That is a strong word, but not too strong: it is in these acts called trivialities that the seeds of joy are forever wasted, until men and women look round with haggard faces at the devastation their own waste has made . . .

George Eliot, *Middlemarch*

Lydia Languish laments, denied her wish to elope with a penniless ensign, since he turns out to be an heir with expectations, and a captain: So becoming a disguise – so amiable a ladder of ropes – conscious moon – four horses – Scotch parson . . . Oh! I shall die of disappointment.

Richard Brinsley Sheridan, The Rivals

If gratitude and esteem are good foundations of affection, Elizabeth's change of sentiment [towards Darcy] will be neither improbable nor faulty. But if otherwise – if the regard springing from such sources is unreasonable or unnatural, in comparison of what is so often described as arising on a first interview with its object, and even before two words have been exchanged – nothing can be said in her defence, except that she had given somewhat of a trial to the latter method in her partiality for Wickham and that its ill success might, perhaps, authorize her to seek the other less interesting mode of attachment.

Jane Austen, Pride and Prejudice

Wickham has, of course, turned out to be the villain of the piece.

Authors

Before condemning the vanity of authors (as I do every day) one should reflect that it is pretty well all they have to sustain them in their lonely task, and that it is present in the great no less than in the minor.

The publisher Rupert Hart-Davis, 1959

O the graceless guineas! It's not so much money I want, but its lack, that's the devil. Is there no mad publisher nowhere?

Walter de la Mare, 1899

How the faithful biographer completed his life's work: he found the Master's lost diary, the secret love letters, the suppressed novel, and the marvellous sonnets in their silk-bound notebook. But a last note was attached: 'If you betray me, I will curse you.' So he burned the papers. Soon after, the insidious hauntings and terminal Alzheimer's began.

Richard Holmes, the distinguished biographer
of Shelley and Coleridge

Richard Holmes, arriving to speak at the Hay Literary Festival on a very muddy day, was greeted with the words, 'Ah, Mr Holmes, perfect biographer's weather. Everywhere we look, feet of clay.'

In biography, and in the literary appraisal of all but the very greatest writers, it is always perfectly simple to make your subject appear a fool – if you want to. All writers, poets especially, write too much, and few of them seem to have any capacity to discriminate between what is good in their work, and what isn't; while it is in the essential nature of human beings – with which species we are obliged to classify even the great Victorians – to be frequently ridiculous.

Morchard Bishop (Oliver Stonor, novelist and man of letters, 1903–87), from his introduction to his (unpublished) book on Arthur Hugh Clough

It had been a busy week and I had wanted a few days' quiet, and exemption from the thought and contrivance which any sort of company gives . . . Composition seems to me impossible with a head full of joints of mutton and doses of rhubarb.

Jane Austen, whose brother Edward had been staying

East Hertfordshire Bus Stations could not have been written without the help of so many wonderful people. Undying thanks go to Mrs Pellew, who taught me to read, an age ago. Arthur Danvers's majestic *Bedfordshire Bus Stations* first lit the flame for me. Thanks to Dawn Gillingham for courage, confidence and cocoa, and to Terry Bassett – you always could spell better than me, Terry! Sid Alton laid down his cloak for me when the puddles were getting too big. Away from Hertfordshire, Lao-tzu taught me that a journey of 1,000 miles must begin with one step, and Ludwig Wittgenstein's *Tractatus Logico-Philosophicus* was invaluable, as always. My debt to Phyllis Dobson cannot be repaid this side of the grave. Gerry, my gerbil, was always there for me, even when humans weren't. Tony Blair made me proud to be British. And, eternally, of course, thanks to huggybun – just because.

Nicholas Hodgson's entry for the *Spectator* competition No. 2,284, which asked for imaginary Acknowledgements pages

The 'misery memoir', a genre that hovers uncomfortably but profitably between therapy for the author and emotional pornography for the reader

Peter Parker in *Slightly Foxed,* Spring 2016

Reading fiction extends your experience of people and emotion, it helps with your knowledge both of the world you are in and of yourself, because you recognize things that matter, that you have not quite grasped. It's difficult to recognize things unless they have been named: fiction names them. The other reason fiction matters is this: it is traditionally quite concerned with morals, so when you are reading it you are exercising your mind in a moral dimension.

The novelist Isabel Colegate in an interview

When I find myself doing ill or like to come to a stand-still in writing I take up some slight book, a novel or the like, and usually have not read far ere my difficulties are removed and I am ready to write again. There must be two currents of ideas going on in my mind at the same time, or perhaps the slighter occupation serves . . . to ballast the mind . . . and so give the deeper current the power to flow undisturbed.

The half-hour between waking and rising has all my life proved propitious to any task which was exercising my invention . . . This is so much the case, that I am in the habit of saying to myself when I am at a loss, 'Never mind, we shall have it at seven o'clock tomorrow morning.'

Sir Walter Scott on writer's block, from his *Journal*

The Gentry

Two definitions of a gentleman:
The hereditary characteristics of a country squire, namely considerable ignorance, under the guidance and direction of strong prejudice, without any mixture of deliberate malignity whatsoever
The English Chronicle, c. 1780

Someone who can make a grouse do for six
Nigel Nicolson, according to his son Adam,
author of a book entitled *The Gentry,* 2012

As for gentlemen, they be made good cheap in England.
Sir Thomas Smith, *De Republica Anglorum,* 1583

Christ was a gentleman of blood, according to his humanity . . .
and might if he had esteemed of the vainglory of the world . . . have
borne coat-armour.
Sir John Frere, *The Blazon of Gentry,* 1586

At meals [in a gentleman's house] you shall have a scattered troop of dishes, led in by some black puddings, and in the rear some demolished pastys which are not yet fallen to the serving man. Between meals there be bread and beer for all comers, and for a stranger a napkin and cold meat in the buttery may be obtained. All the rooms smell of dogs and hawks, and the hall bears arms, though it be but a musket and two corselets . . . The master of the house is adored as a relic of gentility . . . His house is the seat of hospitality, the poor man's court of justice, the curate's Sunday ordinary [dinner], and the only exchequer of charity.
Wye Saltonstall, *Picturae Loquentes,* 1631

There is nothing appears to me more ridiculous or more nearly allied to a vulgar spirit than what I meet with in most gentlemen of England, namely a vain affectation to fly beyond the Moon and to credit themselves (as they think) with long and fictitious pedigrees.

Gervase Holles, *Memorials of the Holles Family*, 1650s

The power of the 17th-century gentry was sanctioned by violence – riding out against their enemies, hamstringing their neighbours' dogs, beating their farmers' sons, or shooting down their riotous labourers. They played ducks and drakes with the law when it suited them, breaking what they were supposed to maintain.

J. H. Plumb, *The Growth of Political Stability in England, 1675–1725*

'Hanging mad dogs, swearing bastards, convicting poachers' – the radical MP and brewer Samuel Whitbread called these 'the usual country occupations', meaning for a gentleman justice of the peace.

The Creevey Papers, 1808

She always addressed an attorney by letter as Mister, raising up her eyebrows when appealed to on the matter, and explaining that an attorney is not an Esquire. She had an idea that a son of a gentleman, if he intended to maintain his rank as a gentleman, should earn his income as a clergyman, or a barrister, or a soldier or a sailor. These were the professions intended for gentlemen. She would not absolutely say that a physician was not a gentleman or even a surgeon, but she would never allow to Physic the same absolute privilege which, in her eyes, belonged to the Law or the Church. There might also be a doubt about the Civil Service and Civil Engineering, but she had no doubt whatever that when a man touched trade or commerce in any way he was doing that which was not the work of a gentleman. He might be very respectable and it might be very interesting that he should do it, but brewers, bankers and merchants were not gentlemen and the world, according to Miss Marrable's theory, was gone astray, because people were forgetting their landmarks.

Anthony Trollope, *The Vicar of Bullhampton,* 1870

Anxieties about the position of the professional and commercial middle classes in the social scale remained strong throughout the nineteenth century. Trollope, unsure of his own status, obviously made a close study of the subject. An attorney is today's solicitor. For more of Trollope on the *same, see p. 87.*

By 1943 Keith Douglas was composing his famous poem, entitled 'Aristocrats', but really about the gentry, his fellow-officers in the Sherwood Rangers Yeomanry, who had only given up their horses for tanks three years before.

How can I live among this gentle
obsolescent breed of heroes, and not weep?
Unicorns, almost,
for they are fading into two legends
in which their stupidity and chivalry
are celebrated. Each, fool and hero, will be immortal.

Russia

In 1898 the Emperor and Empress came to dinner one night at the Embassy, which made the Ambassador Sir Nicholas O'Conor very proud, as it was the only foreign house he so honoured that year. We sat down 42 . . . The whole dinner was sent from Paris, and great consternation had been caused because an accident took place on the railway line. However it arrived just in time. The Emperor and Empress were served on gold plate. The Grand Duchess Vladimir had a bottle of wine spilt down her back, but later in the evening, when signing her name in the book, she managed to get her own back by upsetting a bottle of ink over Lady O'Conor. We danced to a balalaika band, who said they would play either for nothing, or for £200. About 250 people came to the dance, which I believe cost the Ambassador nearly £2,000.

The reminiscences of Sir Thomas Hohler, *Diplomatic Petrel*
Later that year the Russian Foreign Secretary, Prince Muraviev, lied to Sir Nicholas so blatantly that his position became untenable and he had to be recalled. Did the £2,000 include the price of the dinner?

In the electricity and heat of love for man there is something greater than chastity and abstinence from meat. War is evil and legal justice is an evil, but it does not follow that I ought to wear bark shoes and sleep on the stove.

Anton Chekhov
His target was Tolstoy's cranky beliefs and exaltation of the peasant.

Rachmaninov, Gorky and Chaliapin were all in the audience at the first performance of *The Cherry Orchard* in January 1904.

We cannot behave like the Tsarist government and punish people for a crime already committed. Our job is to anticipate.

A Cheka (secret police) interrogator, soon after the Revolution

A Russian looking at a picture of Adam and Eve: 'No food, no clothes, and they think they're in paradise – just like Russia.'

A prison sentence 'without the right of correspondence' – NKVD (1930s secret police) code for the fact that the person sentenced had already been executed

When Khrushchev denounced Stalin at the 1956 Party Congress secret session, a delegate shouted out, 'Why did you not speak out while all this was going on?' 'Who said that?' demanded Khrushchev. There was silence. 'Now', said Khrushchev, 'you know why not.'

All those who have dealt with the Russians over the centuries have commented on their indifference to the truth. The lie in Russia has indeed become an art form. Russia is an epic country . . . because it is the land where the lie has been erected into a principle of conduct . . . Because Russia has always been a land of villains it is also the land of heroes and saints.

The British Ambassador Sir Roderick Braithwaite's valedictory dispatch on leaving Moscow in 1992

Clever, Clever

Avoid clichés like the plague.

What's another word for thesaurus?

There are two rules about stand-up comedy. The first is always leave them wanting more . . .

Some crossword clues and answers
HIJKLMNO: water (H to O)
Ca?: Manx
Revo: overturned
014: double agent
Kiss me, Hardy: pecking order
Tarry rope: stay
–IST: capitalist
Number: anaesthetist
6+6−9 = food: viands (−ix)
Ebb: wolf

Dim sum ergo non cogito.
   Polymath, book dealer and author of the Remainders column in
   The Times Literary Supplement Eric Korn's take on Descartes' *Cogito*
   ergo sum, 'I think therefore I am'

There's the agnostic dyslexic insomniac who stays up all night wondering if there really is a dog, and the poor soul who asks, 'Am I a bestial sadistic necrophiliac or am I just flogging a dead horse?'

Eternity, the Universe

It is enough for us that [the Universe] has intelligence and significance inside of it, for it has produced us, and that our manifest destiny is to do our damnedest because we want to and because we have to let off our superfluous energy . . . It satisfies our superlatives and it seems to me unnecessary to demand of the Cosmos an assurance that to it also our best is superlative. It is so in our world and that is as far as we can go.

Mr Justice Holmes of the US Supreme Court, 1925

A circle whose centre is everywhere and whose circumference is nowhere

Nicholas of Cusa's (1401–64) definition of God

God endures forever, and is everywhere present; and by existing always and everywhere, He constitutes Duration and Space.

Sir Isaac Newton

The Milky Way, our galactic home, contains up to 400 billion stars and a diameter up to 180,000 light years across. Earth is about 27,000 light years from its centre. In October 2017 the Hubble Telescope raised the total number of galaxies observable to 2 trillion. The Sun and its planets formed from interstellar gas 4.55 billion years ago. The Cosmos of which the Milky Way and all other galaxies are part emerged or 'began' 13.8 billion years ago. But what went on before this 'beginning'?

A colossal explosion has very recently been detected, based on low-frequency radio data. It is the biggest since the Big Bang at the start of the Universe. This 'giant radio fossil' is thought to emanate from a super-massive black hole some 390 million light years from Earth.

Music and Musicians

The thoughts that are expressed to me by music that I love are not too indefinite to be put into words but, on the contrary, too definite.

Felix Mendelssohn

Beethoven spoke to God; God spoke to Mozart.

The year 1893 saw the first performances of Sibelius's Karelia Suite, Dvorak's New World Symphony, Tchaikovsky's Pathétique Symphony, Humperdinck's opera *Hansel and Gretel*, Puccini's opera *Manon Lescaut* and Verdi's opera *Falstaff.*

Sir Georg Solti on Wagner: 'If he can write music like that, he can kill me.'

The British don't like music very much, but they do like the noise it makes.

Sir Thomas Beecham

Beecham was rehearsing the Huddersfield Choral Society in the *Messiah.* He exhorted the ladies, in reference to 'For unto us a child is born' – 'Think rather of the joys of conception than the pains of childbirth.' There was a shocked silence until he followed by saying, 'And then the gentlemen come in with "Wonderful".'

Sir Charles Mackerras on BBC Radio 4, November 1998

Eric Satie had a large collection of outlandish umbrellas. Dvorak was a keen train-spotter.

'Herr Deller, you are eunuch!' 'Madam, I think you mean unique.'

Alfred Deller, the counter-tenor, answers a German lady

The cello is a lovely thing, the Rembrandt of the orchestra, don't you think?

George Lyttelton in jest, to Rupert Hart-Davis

Four rational people conversing – Goethe's description of a string quartet

In 1824 Lady Granville was a guest of George IV at the Royal Pavilion in Brighton. Rossini was one of her fellow-guests.
The King all graciousness to him. He sang, which went to our musical hearts, 'Otello' and 'Figaro', etc. but the courtiers and the rest of the society were indignant at his familiarity. Being fat and lazy, and consequently averse to standing, he took a chair and sat by the King, who however, gave him the kindest reception, and less petit than his suite, understood the man, and treated him as his enthusiasm for music disposed him to do. I hope to hear more of him, for it is an unspeakable pleasure.

Sir Thomas Browne

A Norwich physician (1605–82) and an ornate prose stylist

From *Urn Burial:*
Time which antiquates antiquities, and hath art to make dust of all things . . . Pyramids, arches, obelisks were but the irregularities of vainglory, and wild enormities of ancient magnanimity.

From *The Garden of Cyrus:*
For though discursive enquiry and rational conjecture may leave handsome gashes and flesh-wounds, yet without conjunction of this expect no mortal or dispatching blows unto error.

From *Christian Morals:*
Strive not to run like Hercules, a furlong in a breath; festination may prove precipitation; deliberating delay may be wiser cunctation, and slowness no slothfulness.

Measure not thyself by thy morning shadow, but by the extent of thy grave, and reckon thyself above the earth by the line thou must be contented with under it.

Attend with patience the uncertainty of things, and what lieth yet unexerted in the chaos of futurity.

Though the world be histrionical, and most men live ironically, yet be thou what thou singly art, and personate only thyself.

To ruminate upon evils, to make critical notes upon injuries, and to be too acute in their apprehensions, is to add unto our own tortures, to feather the arrows of our enemies . . .

From *Religio Medici:*
There is surely a piece of Divinity in us, something that was before the Elements, and owns no homage to the Sun.

Elizabeth I

To Parliament at the start of her reign:
What credit my assurance shall deserve to have, the sequel shall declare.

To an ambassador:
Had I been crested not cloven you would not have dared write to me thus.

To Parliament, refusing its wish that she declare a successor:
I am your anointed Queen. I will never be by violence constrained to do anything. I thank God I am endowed with such qualities that if I were turned out of the realm in my petticoat I were able to live in any place in Christendom.

The Queen in state at Greenwich in 1598, seen by Paul Hentzer, tutor to a Silesian nobleman on a tour of England:
Very majestic; her face oblong, fair, but wrinkled; her eyes small, yet black and pleasant; her nose a little hooked; her lips narrow, and her teeth black (a defect the English seem subject to, from their too great use of sugar); she had in her ears two pearls, with very rich drops; she wore false hair, and that red . . . her bosom uncovered as all English ladies have it till they marry.

She walks much in her privy chamber, and stamps with her feet at ill news, and thrusts her rusty sword at times into the arras in great rage . . . The dangers [of Essex's rebellion] are over, and yet she keeps a sword by her table.

A letter of Sir John Harrington, October 1601

To Parliament at the end of her reign:
Assure yourself that the shining glory of princely authority hath not dazzled the eyes of our understanding, but that we well know and remember that we are to yield an account of our actions before the great judge.

You have lived to see the trim of old times, and what passed in the Queen's days. These things are no more the same. Your Queen did talk of her subjects' love and good affections, and in good truth she aimed well. Our King talketh of his subjects' fear and subjection, and herein I think he doth well too, as long as it holdeth good.

    Thomas, Lord Howard in about 1607, of James I, to Harrington

History

In no exact sense does history repeat itself. But the flux in human affairs is constant, and as the spiral unfolds, so are similar problems posed to different men with different capacities and desires. 'The great and exemplary wheels of heaven' revolve, and we who watch them are brought to contemplate afresh the marriage between Time and the Hour.

> David C. Douglas, an outstanding historian of the Normans, in an essay on the Hundred Years War. The quotation in the third sentence is by Sir Thomas Browne (see p. 61)

Mark Twain also believed history did not repeat itself, but rather that it rhymed.

Charles V is a mere hook to hang history upon – Luther is the soul of *that* time.

> The Victorian historian J. R. Green on the 1520s–30s

What I am aware of in Gibbon is precisely what I am aware of in myself, an unceasing compulsion to get the historic particulars into a causal pattern, and then lodge that pattern, once achieved, in a context of related patterns.

> G. M. Young, *Gibbon*, 1932

I often think it odd that history should be so dull, since a great deal of it must be invention.

> Catherine Morland in Jane Austen's *Northanger Abbey*

It is the easiest method of writing history well to people it with complete heroes and authentic villains. Not only are such characters artistically invaluable when found, but the discovery of them is actually assisted by the restful process of ignoring evidence. The task of examining evidence is irksome, and its reward is the risk of losing one's hero and almost the certainty of losing one's villain.

F. A. Simpson, *Louis Napoleon and the Recovery of France*, 1923

All history is geography.

Anon.

There is a kind of alchemy about figures which transforms the most dubious materials into something pure and precious, hence the price of working with historical statistics is eternal vigilance.

Thomas Carlyle

Progressive historians wishing always to remake the sacred into the profane . . . to see motives of class and economics behind every professed sentiment

Deirdre McCloskey, author of the *Bourgeois Era* trilogy

Patronage of the past is a very naïf attitude, apt to go with too simple expectations of the future.

A. L. Rowse

The past was not a rehearsal for the present.

Hilary Mantel

We exist in and for our own time: why should we judge our predecessors as if they were less self-sufficient: as if they existed for us and should be judged by us?

Hugh Trevor-Roper, 'History and Sociology',
Past and Present, 42 (1968)

Can we really be fair to men of the past, knowing what they could not know? Can we indeed understand them at all . . . with our minds prepossessed by the result?

'Tudor Historian' quoted by David Lowenthal
in *History Today,* November 2015

He who knows where he comes from, knows where he is going, for he knows where he is.

Otto von Habsburg, the last Crown Prince of
Austria-Hungary, d. 2011

Emily Eden

Emily Eden was one of the fourteen children of the statesman and diplomat Lord Auckland. Though remembered for her time in India, her natural habitat was the houses of the Grand Whiggery. In 1817, aged 20, she began a letter to one of her sisters:

Indeed, nobody but an excellent sister could be induced to write on such a gloomy, dispiriting afternoon, but I have put the table close to the fire, with one leg (belonging to the table, not to me) in the fender, to prevent it from slipping away, the armchair close behind the table, and me supported by them both, holding my pen in one hand and the poker in the other, and now, have at you.

In 1834 she wrote to a grandmother commiserating on yet another grandchild:

I think it would be such a good plan if, after people have as many children as they like, they were allowed to lie-in of any other article they fancied better; with some pain and trouble of course (if necessary), but the result would be more agreeable. A set of Walter Scott's novels, or some fine china, or in the case of poor people, fire-irons and a coal scuttle, or two pieces of Irish linen.

Miss Eden's Letters, 1919

From 1836 she was in India together with her sister Fanny, supporting their brother, Lord Auckland, the Governor-General, since he had no wife and they were unmarried. Her fame rests on the series of letters she wrote to friends and relations in England from there, the bulk of them to be found in that classic of the Raj, Up the Country *(1866). Here, she writes of the particular quality and value of a letter, something almost entirely lost to us today:*

It is very odd what extraordinary interest those few scratches of a black liquid on a white pulp can give, because the same number of words said in conversation would go a very little way; and yet one folds up a letter with an air of pompous satisfaction, and says,

'Ah! It is very comfortable to know all they have been about' – a deception, only I do not mean to see through it.

She was amazed, in particular, at finding herself living for many months under canvas as she travelled across India, and at the British in India, in general:
How people who might, by economy and taking in washing and plain work, have a comfortable back attic in the neighbourhood of Manchester Square, with a fireplace and a boarded floor, can come and march about India, I cannot guess.

On the palace of the Mogul emperors in Delhi:
A melancholy sight – so magnificent originally, and so poverty-stricken now . . . All our servants were in a state of profound veneration; the natives all look upon the King of Delhi as their rightful lord, and so he is, I suppose. In some of the pavilions belonging to the princes there were such beautiful inlaid floors, any square of which would have made an enviable table for a palace in London, but the stones are constantly stolen; and in some of the finest baths there were dirty charpoys spread, with dirtier guards sleeping on them. In short, Delhi is a very suggestive and moralising place – such stupendous remains of power and wealth passed and passing away – and somehow I feel we horrid English have just 'gone and done it', merchandised it, revenued it, and spoiled it all. I am not very fond of Englishmen out of their own country.

At Simla in the foothills of the Himalayas where the British went to escape the summer heat:
The Queen's Ball 'came off' yesterday with great success . . . Twenty years ago no European had ever been here, and there we were,

with the band playing the 'Puritani' and 'Masaniello', and eating salmon from Scotland, and sardines from the Mediterranean, and observing that [her brother's French chef] St Cloup's *potage à la julienne* was perhaps better than other soups, and some of the ladies' sleeves were too tight according to the overland fashions for March, etc.; and all this in the face of those high hills, some of which have remained untrodden since the Creation, and we, 105 Europeans, being surrounded by at least 3,000 mountaineers, who, wrapped up in their hill blankets, looked on at what we call polite amusements, and bowed to the ground if a European came near them. I sometimes wonder they do not cut all our heads off, and say nothing more about it.

To be sure, an inch of amiability is worth yards of cleverness for the real wear and tear of life.

Gardens and Parks

An old yew tree: 'made to unedge the scythe of time'

Francis Thompson

. . . a lawn delicious to one's sentient boot . . .

Henry James

There is not a leaf big enough to cover a caterpillar's pudenda.

Horace Walpole on a late Spring

I feel when I set out to walk as if alone in the world – nothing but trees and birds, but then comes the enormous satisfaction of finding a man dressing a hedge or a woman in a gingham [apron] and a black bonnet on her knees picking up weeds.

Lady Granville on her brother-in-law,
the Marquess of Stafford's, gardens at Trentham

Shows what God could have done if he'd had the money.

The New Yorker writer Wolcott Gibbs's comment on the hugely
expensive transplanting of a full-sized elm tree to some rich man's garden

Every garden, however small, should include at least two acres of rough woodland.

The 1st Lord Rothschild

Monet had six gardeners at Giverny. One did nothing but dead-head flowers; another spent his days in a boat weeding the pond.

I should like now to promenade you round gardens – apple-tasting – pear-tasting – plum-judging – apricot-nibbling – peach-scrunching – nectarine-sucking and melon-carving – I have also a great feeling for antiquated cherries full of sugar cracks – and a white currant tree kept for company.

John Keats to Fanny Keats, 1819

The origin of gazebo: gazeabout

The Torrington Diaries, Chepstow, 1781

> . . . the skulking sly ha-ha,
> By whose miraculous assistance
> You gain a prospect two fields' distance.

The Connoisseur, August 1756

Now the black trees in Regent's Park opposite are beginning to show green buds; and men come by with great baskets of flowers, primroses, hepaticas, crocuses, great daisies etc, calling as they go, 'Growing, growing! All the glory going!'

Edward Fitzgerald, *Letters*, 1857

> My very heart faints and my whole soul grieves
> At the moist rich smell of the rotting leaves,
> And the breath
> Of the fading edges of box beneath,
> And the year's last rose.
> Heavily hangs the broad sunflower
> Over its grave i'the earth so chilly;
> Heavily hangs the hollyhock,
> Heavily hangs the tiger-lily.

Tennyson, from his 'Song', 1831

Tennyson thought an English gentleman's park in May the most beautiful sight on earth.

A gentleman's park is my aversion. It is not beauty because it is not nature.

John Constable

The Duke of Argyll announced he wanted to die before Capability Brown so that he could see the Elysian Fields before he had improved them.

Now Mellicant, you and I can do here what we please.

George III to the under-gardener at Richmond,
on the news of the death of Capability Brown in 1783

Oft when I've seen some lonely mansion stand,
Fresh from th' improver's desolating hand,
'Midst shaven lawns, that far around it creep
In one eternal undulating sweep . . .
To Heaven devoutly I've addressed my prayer,
Again the moss-grown terraces to raise,
And spread the labyrinth's perplexing maze;
Replace in even lines the ductile yew,
And plant again the ancient avenue.

Richard Payne Knight, *The Landscape*, 1794

Opera

Don Giovanni should have married Carmen.

Walter Raleigh

Casanova was in the audience at the first performance of *Don Giovanni*, in Prague in 1787. Mozart's librettist, Lorenzo da Ponte, met Casanova there, but neglected his advice not to gamble in London so was forced to become a grocer in New York.

Massinet's opera *Thaïs* had its première in Paris in 1894. In it a courtesan fails to seduce a monk. Later the monk has renounced his vows while she has found God, so when he in turn tries to seduce her, she refuses and then dies as the final curtain falls. At that point a voice from the gallery shouted, '*Vite. Alors qu'elle est toujours tiède.*' – 'Quick. Now while she's still warm.'

In an idiotic production of Meyerbeer's *Les Huguenots* at Covent Garden in 1992, when a woman member of the cast stripped, a voice from the gods shouted, 'Get 'em on!'

The original of Dumas' *Dame aux Camellias* and therefore of Verdi's *La Traviata*, Alphonsine Plessis, got married at Kensington Registry Office to Edouard de Perregaux but soon deserted him for the owner of Château Margaux. She died, aged 23, in 1847.

At the first night of *The Barber of Seville* in 1816 a singer fell off the stage and a cat wandered on to it. Thereafter the audience made mewing sounds throughout. Afterwards a mortified Rossini locked himself in a dressing-room. He is supposed to have composed the opera in only 13 days – or at least those passages not lifted from his earlier operas. The following year he composed *La Cenerentola* in three weeks, still only aged 25.

Emilia di Liverpool was the title of one of Donizetti's early operas.

Molière pointed out that of all the noises known to man, opera is the most expensive.

An old-fashioned producer said in 2007 that as far as *The Marriage of Figaro* is concerned, 'As long as you get the doors in the right places, the rest doesn't matter.'

Claire Tomalin, that marvellous literary biographer, says at the end of her memoir *A Life of My Own* (2017), that sitting in an opera house and hearing the opening of the overture to *The Marriage of Figaro* represents perfect happiness for her.

The First World War

Some premonitions
In 1863 the future Kaiser Wilhelm II, aged 4, wore Highland dress at the wedding of his uncle, the Prince of Wales. He brandished his dirk and threw his sporran into the choir.

The day before becoming Foreign Secretary in June 1870, Lord Granville was briefed by the Permanent Under Secretary, who said, 'He had never, during his long experience, known so great a lull in foreign affairs.' At six o'clock that evening Granville 'received a telegram informing me of the choice which had been made by . . . Spain of Prince Leopold of Hohenzollern, and of his acceptance of the offer [of the Spanish Crown].'
As Bismarck intended, France was provoked by the prospect of branches of the Hohenzollern family ruling two large countries to either side of her, and this led to the outbreak of the Franco-Prussian War, the crushing defeat of France, which lost Alsace and Lorraine, followed by the unification of Germany under a Hohenzollern emperor.

> Again the guns disturbed the hour,
> Roaring their readiness to avenge,
> As far inland as Stourton Tower,
> And Camelot, and starlit Stonehenge.
>> The last verse of Thomas Hardy's poem
>> 'Channel Firing', written in April 1914

Some statistics
About 12 per cent of the British armed forces in the war died; the same percentage died in the Napoleonic Wars.

Two-thirds of the nine and a half million fatalities on all fronts were killed by shell fire.

Four million horses were killed on the Western Front.

The 21st March 1918, the first day of the great German Spring offensive, Operation Michael, was the day of highest losses in the war, when 78,000 men were killed, wounded or taken prisoner.

* * *

I never saw anything like the foulness and desolation of this bit of the [Ypres] Salient. There were two woods near to us in which we roamed about picking up gruesome relics in the dusk – Maple Copse and Sanctuary Wood – not a leaf or a blade of grass in either of them, nothing but twisted and blackened stumps and a mesh of shell holes, dimpling into one another, full of mud and blood, and dead men and over-fed rats which blundered into one in the twilight like fat moths.

Raymond Asquith to his wife in June 1916, *Letters*, 1980
Eldest son of the Prime Minister, he served in the Grenadier Guards and was killed later that year.

Speaking in Washington in 1941, Churchill went counterfactual:
America's entry into the 1914–18 War was disastrous not only for your country but for the Allies as well because had you stayed at home . . . we would have made peace in the Spring of 1917 and then there would have been no collapse of Russia, followed by Communism, no breakdown of Italy, followed by Fascism, and Nazism would not be at present enthroned in Germany.

The Second World War

A 'What if'

In 1931 the late Lord Howard de Walden was staying in Munich in the gap between school and university when a man stepped off the pavement as he drove along in his small Fiat. The man was knocked over but got up immediately and dusted himself down. After Howard de Walden had driven off again, his German companion explained whom he had hit: Adolf Hitler.

Some statistics

There were more deaths on British roads in the first two years of the war than in the armed forces, because of the blackout. The first RAF combat losses of the war were two Hurricanes, shot down by Spitfires.

At the de Havilland works at Edgware 4,426 days were lost in August 1940 over 'the transfer of four capstan fitters from the firm to other work of national importance'. In September some London dockers and Clydeside shipbuilders were on strike.

During the four years of the Occupation of France 200,000 children were conceived with German fathers; in Rouen alone there were something like 4,000. The final twelve months of the war saw an 800 per cent rise in the number of husbands suing for divorce on the grounds of adultery in Britain.

Britain lost 379,762 combatants killed and 475,000 wounded, plus 65,000 civilians. The United States lost 292,100 killed and 571,822 wounded, with negligible civilian casualties. Russia had a combined total, military and civilian, of 27 million dead. British and American ground troops killed about 200,000 German soldiers; the Russians more than 3 million.

Politics and Politicians

In 1679 the Habeas Corpus Bill passed the House of Lords by 57 to 55 votes, but there were only 107 peers attending. Lord Norris, a teller for the Bill's supporters, had counted the inordinately fat Lord Grey as ten votes, not one.

The Duke of Newcastle made his entry with as much alacrity and noise as usual, mightily out of breath, though mightily in words, and in his hand a bundle of papers as big as his head and with little more in them.

Lord Hervey, Memoirs, 1733

He may have been a figure of fun, but he was also a most effective politician for four decades or more.

I left Fox and Grey at ten o'clock just beginning to talk thick.

Lord Minto, 1790

A steady patriot of the world alone,
The friend of every country but his own.

George Canning, from his satire 'New Morality',
in the Anti-Jacobin, 1798, mocking the multiculturalists

If he were a horse, nobody would buy him.

Walter Bagehot, the political journalist, on the look in the eyes of
Henry Brougham, the radical politician and Lord Chancellor

Palmerston always put Canning in mind of a footman who thought his mistress was in love with him; but *who was mistaken.*

Lord Hatherton

Lord Grey told William IV that the Great Reform Bill 'would operate rather favourably than otherwise for the landed interest.' Sure enough, the first thing his government did after it passed was to create two new dukes.

Damn the Whigs, they're all cousins.

Sir Robert Peel, 1834

Damn the Tories, they're dullards, and it wins them votes.

Lord Palmerston

Queen Victoria said of Lord John Russell that he would be better company if he had a third subject; for he was interested in nothing except the constitution of 1688 and – himself.

Much is made of Attlee sending the distinguished judge Cyril Radcliffe to Delhi in 1947 and allotting him five weeks in which to delineate the new boundary between India and Pakistan. But there is a precedent. Some months into the Indian Mutiny in 1857 Palmerston asked Lord Clarendon, his Foreign Secretary, to think about what sort of government should be established there, to replace the East India Company, once peace returned. He suggested Clarendon could do this 'while I am shaving or walking'.

Either Lord Aberdeen or Lord Palmerston was Foreign Secretary or Prime Minister in all the years between 1828 and 1865.

Disraeli observed that the trouble with Mr Gladstone was that he had not a single redeeming defect.

Here they come, low and weaving like Tories.

The 9th Duke of Devonshire,
true to his Whig ancestry,
on the birds flying towards his grouse butt

Arthur Balfour viewed events 'with the detachment of a choirboy at a funeral service'.

Lord Vansittart

If you can't ride two horses at once, you shouldn't be working in the circus.

Jimmy Maxton, Red Clydeside MP between the wars

I feel we should not give him a post at this stage. Anything he undertakes he puts his heart and soul into. If there is going to be a war – and no one can say that there is not – we must keep him fresh to be our war Prime Minister.

Prime Minister Stanley Baldwin about Churchill in 1935, to J. C. C. Davidson

Worse even than bridge, elections combine stupefying boredom with bursts of activity ending often in humiliation.

Jo Grimond, for many years leader of the Liberals

Always keep in with those out.
Never get between a dog and a lamp-post.
Never believe anything until it has been officially denied.

Some political guidelines in the Middle East by Stewart Perowne, Arabist, archaeologist, author and, improbably, husband of Freya Stark

Doing away with tradition is not in itself a reform.
A report is not necessarily more true because it is marked 'top secret'.

Some more, by Douglas Hurd

Sir Alec Douglas-Home's wife used to repeat, as they went down the aeroplane steps, 'China, Alec, China' (or wherever), to remind him which country they had got to on their foreign tour.

Ted Heath very much fancied himself as a conductor. During rehearsals with a professional orchestra, his comments became increasingly curt. Finally the leader of the orchestra said, 'If you don't stop being so rude to us, Sir Edward, we may start obeying your instructions.'

President Mitterrand famously said Mrs Thatcher had '*les yeux de Caligule et la bouche de Marilyn Monroe*'. Chris Patten called her the boa constrictor in the chandelier.

At the opening of Tate Modern in 2000, Tony Blair told the novelist Ian McEwan that he had several of his works hanging on his walls.

Some Places

Kent and Surrey
If Kent is the Garden of England, Surrey must be the patio.

Michael Bracewell on BBC2, April 1997

Kent, Sir – everybody knows Kent – apples, cherries, hops, and women. Glass of wine, Sir?

Mr Jingle in Dickens, Pickwick Papers

Derbyshire
Not mountainous enough to please one with its horrors

Thomas Gray, 1762

Some people might think it verging on the extreme of picturesque and call it wild.

Emily Eden, 1824

Warwickshire
The landscape indeed sins by excess of nutritive suggestion; it savours of larder and manger; it is too ovine, too bovine, it is almost asinine; and if you were to believe what you see before you this rugged globe would be a sort of boneless ball covered with such plush-like integument as might be figured by the down on the cheek of a peach.

Henry James, English Hours

London
Pimlico: a loosely interpreted, an almost transpontine Belgravia

Henry James, English Hours

A new habit sprang up in the 1850s of women being allowed to walk alone in the new district of Belgravia. Formerly no lady went

out unaccompanied by a servant . . . No lady would have willingly
driven down St James's Street or dreamt of stopping at a club door.

Sir Algernon West, Recollections, 1899

Some insults
Brighton has the air of a town helping the police with their en-
quiries.

Keith Waterhouse

Erith is so miserable it's not even twinned with anywhere, though
it does have a suicide pact with Middlesbrough.

The late Linda Smith, stand-up comedian

She sometimes substituted Rotherham and Scunthorpe, or Braintree
for Middlesbrough.

Middlesbrough: the Soviet Union with take-away pizza

Anthony Daniels

In 2017 a local academic's research established that the age at which
young persons from Middlesbrough resign themselves to the fact that
they are never going to be able to do anything with their lives is not
18, not 16, but 9.

Manchester: the only town where there's lifeboat drill on the buses

Les Dawson

Royalty

In the 1930s some royal mummies were transported from the Valley of the Kings to Cairo. One of the Amenhotep pharaohs of the 18th dynasty, from the middle centuries of the second millennium BC, though he still had a garland of flowers round his neck when he was disinterred, travelled by 1st class sleeper, in the top bunk.

It is entirely irrational to ignore the irrational.

Antony Jay on the monarchy

As well as being co-author of Yes Minister *and* Yes, Prime Minister, *he wrote and co-wrote the two outstanding television documentary series,* Royal Family *and* Elizabeth R.

Georg Ludwig, Kurfürst von Braunschweig-Lüneberg, is known to us as George I. When the Royal family's name was changed to Windsor in 1917 the College of Arms could not decide whether it had been Guelph, Wettin or Saxe-Coburg-Gotha. The Duke of Edinburgh's family name is Schleswig-Holstein-Sonderburg-Glucksburg. In 1947 he took his maternal grandfather's name, Mountbatten, anglicized from Battenberg.

Adolphus, Duke of Cambridge, one of George III's many children, replied to the curate's 'Let us pray', in Kew Church in 1842, with an amiable 'By all means.'

Out shooting one day at Sandringham, George V made Queen Mary join in the beating: 'May, r-r-rattle your brollie, r-r-rattle your brollie.' Queen Mary said late in life her one regret was that she had never climbed a fence.

Tommy Lascelles, the King's private secretary, recorded George VI's complaints about some government interference during a train journey: 'Suddenly he threw his arm out at the window and exclaimed, "And that's where it all started!" We were passing Runnymede.'

'Where did you get that hat?'

Princess Margaret to the Queen as she emerged
from her coronation in Westminster Abbey in 1953

'The Queen is the only person who can put on a tiara with one hand while walking downstairs.'

Princess Margaret again

The Queen remarked, after saying they were heavy: 'There are some disadvantages to crowns, but otherwise they are quite important.'

Harold Macmillan claimed to have been greeted once on arrival at Sandringham by the Duke of Gloucester, a brother of George VI: 'Thank heavens you've come, Prime Minister. The Queen's in a terrible state; there's a fellow called Jones who wants to marry her sister and Prince Philip's in the library wanting to change the family name to Mountbatten.'

When Clare Short's mobile went off during a meeting of the Privy Council soon after Labour came to power in 1997, the Queen said, 'You'd better answer that. It might be someone important.'

When the late Martin McGuinness, former senior IRA figure but then a Northern Ireland minister, asked the Queen in 2012 how she was, she said, 'Still alive.'

The Aristocracy

The 1st Marquis of Abercorn (d. 1818) always wore his Garter ribbon out shooting and required his housemaids to wear white kid gloves when they made his bed.

The Aga Khan is held by his followers to be the direct descendant of God. English dukes take precedence.

The ruling of the College of Arms

The Aga Khan, believed to be a direct descendant of the Prophet (not God), is the spiritual head of the 15 million Ismaili Muslims, and his family are of immense wealth.

On finding the Chapel Royal full, one of her daughters asked the 1st Marchioness of Salisbury (d. 1835), 'Where shall we go, Mama?' 'Home again, to be sure. If we cannot get in, it is no fault of ours – we have done the civil thing.'

At Snaith (Yorkshire) they had got pretty well on in the service when the Vicar made a solemn pause: on turning round Lord and Lady Downe were to be seen, followed by a footman carrying an array of prayer-books and other comforts, walking with slow and stately pace up the aisle. As they approached the pulpit the Vicar made a profound bow, which was most politely returned by Lord Downe, who then entered the family pew and reverently placed his face, as was then the custom, within his hat; then having comfortably seated themselves and calmly found the places in their books, the service, which had been completely suspended, was allowed to proceed.

From the mid-1820s:

The Letter-Bag of Lady Elizabeth Spencer Stanhope

'Tis an animal incapable of leading a rational life (that is, what we should call so) and quite insufficient to itself. It must always be running after a fox, a hare, a blue ribbon, a place or some such thing, or given up to play [gambling]. I do think nature has given us women the best lot in this queer jumble of life.

Caroline Fox, daughter of the Duke of Richmond, wife of the 1st Lord Holland, mother of Charles James Fox and aunt of Sir Charles Napier (see p. 31), on the aristocratic Englishman of the mid-eighteenth century

George Agar-Ellis, son of Viscount Clifden, was vexed by his failure to produce an heir. Sydney Smith wrote to Lady Holland:
I did not say so – but I thought how absurd to discontinue the use of domestic chaplains where landed property is concerned.

Lady Lufton liked cheerful, quiet well-to-do people, who loved their Church, their country, and their Queen, and who were not too anxious to make a noise in the world. She desired that all the farmers round her should be able to pay their rents without trouble, that all the old women should have warm flannel petticoats, that the working men should be saved from rheumatism by healthy food and dry houses, that they should all be obedient to their pastors and masters – temporal and spiritual. That was her idea of loving her country. She desired also that the copses should be full of pheasants, the stubble fields of partridges, and the gorse covers of foxes; in that way, also, she loved her country. She had ardently longed, during the Crimean War, that the Russians might be beaten – but not by the French, to the exclusion of the English, as had seemed to her to be too much the case; and hardly by the English under the dictatorship of Lord Palmerston.

The Tory paternalist ideal, Anthony Trollope, *Framley Parsonage*, 1860

I have long been addicted to the gaming table. I have lately taken to the Turf. I fear I frequently blaspheme. But I have never distributed religious tracts. All this was known to you and your Society. Notwithstanding which you think me a fit person to be your president. God forgive your hypocrisy.

From the 3rd Earl of Orford's letter in 1824
to the Norwich Bible Society

Virginia Woolf said that, 'To have had the author of the letter among one's ancestors would have been a source of inordinate pride.' In spite of John Julius Norwich having included it in his 2009 Christmas Cracker *I repeat it here since the Earl was one of my wife's sixteen great-great-great-grandfathers. Regret must be mixed in with her pride because in 1856 he sold Rubens's famous* Rainbow Landscape *to the Marquess of Hertford, which is why it is now in the Wallace Collection.*

At the revival of *Lady Windermere's Fan,* I asked Lady Alexander, exquisite as ever and looking like the lids of Juno's eyes, whether in the 1890s peeresses at private dances wore tiaras. She said, 'They wore them at the tea-table!'

James Agate, *Ego,* 1945

The princely family of the Cantacuzenes were categorized by the Communist rulers of Romania after the Second World War as 'elements of putrid background'.

An Oxford scout, a male domestic college servant, remained proud in the 1960s that he had once been the only footman at nearby Blenheim Palace 'to wear my own calves', when dressed in uniform breeches and stockings. The rest required special calf pads to achieve the desired shape of leg.

Printing in the Early Days

It is estimated that there were only 30,000 books in existence before the coming of the printing press.

In 1492 the Abbot of Sponheim, Johannes Trithemius, wrote *In Praise of Scribes* in which he argued against the new printing press. He then got his book printed.

By 1480, twelve years after Gutenberg's death, there were presses in 120 European towns. A single press could produce 200 pages an hour. Five million books had been printed by 1500.

Hernando Colon, son of Christopher Columbus, had collected 15,370 books in his Biblioteca Hernandina in Seville by the time he died in 1539. He had been attempting to form a 'universal library'.

From the epitaph to the 'ingenious and iudicious artist, Mr John Haviland', a printer, in Winstone Church, Gloucestershire, who died in 1638:

> None printed more, and erred lesse in print:
> None led a life that had lesse errors in't . . .
> Well has he finish'd then his pilgrim race,
> Who ever liv'd in forme, and died in case.
> This constant impreze then shall seale his grave
> 'Each yeare my works must new impressions have.'
> A matrice gave me life, a matrice gaine,
> And earth's the matrice that does me containe.

England, Britain

How many British Isles? About 7,700 according to the Ordnance Survey. And 500 mountains (over 2,000 ft), and 300 rivers. In 5000 BC the population was about 5,000; by 1400 BC it had reached 1,000,000.

Shortly after Stonehenge was built in about 2500 BC, samples of DNA from bones show that the population was almost entirely replaced by the 'Beaker People', migrants from Europe named after their distinctive pottery. For the first time Britons had ancestry, skin and eye colour similar to the majority of Britons today.

An important wassail-night, when the two black-browed brothers, strong-headed, headstrong, Hengst and Horsa (*Stallion* and *Horse*), determined on a man-hunt in Britain, the boar-hunt at home having got overcrowded; and so a few hungry Angles made an English Nation, and planted it here, and – produced *thee*, O Reader!

Thomas Carlyle, 'On History Again'
from *Miscellanies*

Rex Totius Anglorum Patriae: King of all the country of the Angles
King Offa of Mercia's title (d. 796)

By 1000 the name Englalond began to be used in the *Anglo-Saxon Chronicle*. In the Provisions of Oxford, of 1258, the first document issued in English in the King's name since the Norman Conquest, Henry III is called King of Engleneloande. In a letter of 1475, the spelling has become Ynklond.

St George was upon his horse, and drew out his sword and garnished him with the sign of the cross, and rode hardily against the dragon which came towards him, and smote him with his spear and hurt him sore and threw him to the ground . . . patron of this realm of England and the cry of men of war.

William Caxton, *The Golden Legend,* 1485

The English are grave like the Germans, lovers of shew . . . They excel in dancing and music, for they are active and lively, though of a thicker make than the French; they cut their hair on the middle of the head, letting it grow on either side; they are good sailors, and better pirates, cunning, treacherous, and thievish; above 300 are said to be hanged annually in London . . . They are powerful in the field, successful against their enemies, impatient of anything like slavery; vastly fond of great noises that fill the ear, such as the firing of cannon, drums, and the ringing of bells, so that in London it is common for a number of them, that have got a glass in their heads, to go up into some belfry, and ring the bells for hours together, for the sake of exercise. If they see a foreigner, very well made or particularly handsome, they will say, 'It is a pity he is not an Englishman.'

Paul Hentzer, a German visitor, 1598 (see p. 62)

'An ill-born amphibious mob.' The English, according to Daniel Defoe

All the way home, I could but gaze at the felicity of my countrymen. The road was one string of stage-coaches, loaded within and without with noisy jolly folks, and chaises and gigs that had been pleasuring in clouds of dust; every door and every window of every house was open, lights in every shop, every door with women sitting in the street, every inn crowded with jaded horses, and every ale-house full of drunken topers; for you know the English always announce their sense of heat or cold by drinking. Well! it was impossible not to enjoy such a scene of happiness and affluence in every village and amongst the lowest of the people; and who are told by villainous scribblers that they are oppressed and miserable . . . How bitter to turn from this Elysium to the Temple [prison] at Paris! The fiends there have now torn her son from the Queen.

Horace Walpole to his cousin Henry Seymour Conway, July 1793
The Queen was Marie Antoinette, who was to be guillotined in October.

The painter Benjamin Robert Haydon (1786–1846) said the reason he didn't leave England was 'its beef, its bottom, and its boxing'.

England should be the terror of the ambitious and the scheming, and the asylum of the oppressed, and that I think is your notion.

One Whig aristocrat, Lord William Russell,
to Lord Holland, another, 1824

The Red Ensign affirmed in its numbers the stability of purpose, the continuity of effort and the greatness of Britain's opportunity pursued steadily in the order and peace of the world: that world which for 25 years or so after 1870 may be said to have been living in holy calm and hushed silence with only now and then a slight clink of metal, as if in some distant part of mankind's habitation some restless body had stumbled over a heap of old armour.

Joseph Conrad, 'Confidence',
in *Notes on Life and Letters,* 1921

After a Polish perspective, three more German views
Great Britain, which cannot naturally be considered, in the balance of Europe, but as belonging to the second order of kingdoms, has been elevated to the rank of one of the first powers in the world by bravery, wealth, liberty, and the happy consequence of an excellent political system.

J. W. von Archenholz, formerly a captain in the service of
the King of Prussia, *A Picture of England,* 1789

If I were not what I am, I would like to be an Englishman.

The young Metternich (b. 1773)

Foreigners think Parliamentarismus a form of government. It is nothing of the kind. It is an English game, like cricket, which only English people can play.

Oswald Spengler, author of *Decline of the West,* 1918, in 1920

Mr Podsnap considered other countries a mistake . . . 'This island was Blest, Sir, to the direct Exclusion of such other countries as – as there may happen to be.'

Charles Dickens, *Our Mutual Friend*

Sex

Prostitute's advertising sticker in a phone box: For sale, large chest

A friend was offered a bedsit in exchange for beating the landlord – something he termed 'light housework'.

Fiona Pitt-Kethley

The licentious Lord Chancellor, Lord Lyndhurst (d. 1863), when asked if he believed in platonic friendships, said, 'After, not before'.

I found the little dog so little that of himself he could not reach our bitch . . . God forgive me, it went against me to have my wife and servants look upon them while they endeavoured to do something, and yet it provoked me to pleasure with my wife more than usual tonight.

Samuel Pepys, 22 March 1664

Woody Allen defended masturbation as sex with someone you love.

A reviewer of *The Bourgeois Experience* by Peter Gay (1998) remarked that 'the onanist panic' which affected Europe in the nineteenth century, reminded him of the witchcraft craze in the sixteenth and seventeenth centuries.

A lady with a jealous husband said to the ageing Duc de Richelieu, 'Monsieur le Duc, fortune has at length thrown the happy moment in our way. My husband is gone and it will take him full five minutes to return.' He replied, *'Mon Dieu, Madame, me-prenez-vous pour un pistolet?'*

The 19th-century novelist Samuel Butler 'had a woman upon whom he vented his appetite, often without troubling to unbutton his trousers'.

James Lees-Milne, *Prophesying Peace*

The Comte d'Aumale was much *épris* with the actress Rachel and sent her a three-word note: *'Quand? Où? Combien?'* To which she replied: *'Demain, chez moi, rien!'*

Lord Clarendon, *Journal*, 31 July 1846

Two men – yes – I can see they have something to get hold of. But two women – that's impossible. You can't have two insides having an affair.

The Russian ballerina Lydia Lopokova, wife of J. M. Keynes

Lilian Baylis, creator of the Old Vic theatre, to the juvenile lead, Eric Portman, in 1928: 'Are you pure, dear boy?' 'I beg your pardon, Miss Baylis?' 'I asked if you were pure.' 'I hope so, Miss Baylis.' 'I am all for everybody having their proper mate in life, but I don't like it going on in the wings.'

The unnatural vice among the men (now so modish) appears to me to owe its vehemence [to the fact that] they cannot talk of this internal torment, so after having glutted their vile imaginations for some time, the senses take alarm and burst out with uncontrolled frenzy: as in Bickerstaff, Onslow and Lady Fanny Burgoyne's footman, who attacked a grave man of fifty years old in a gross manner, even before his lady's face at the chariot door. The Scotch seem strangely addicted to this enormity, and 'tis a cold country too.

I can think of no reason but one – their wearing fillibegs [kilts].'

Mrs Thrale, writing in the eighteenth century, *Thraliana*

Now the world is networked, and ideas are having sex with each other more promiscuously than ever, the pace of innovation will redouble.

Matt Ridley, *The Rational Optimist*, 2010

As [the Gnostics] were, for the most part, averse to the pleasures of sense, they morosely arraigned the polygamy of the patriarchs, the gallantries of David, and the seraglio of Solomon.

Edward Gibbon, *The Decline and Fall of the Roman Empire*, chapter 15

Horace Walpole tells the story of the Duke of Beaufort who wanted a divorce from his wife because of her affair with Lord Talbot. She defended herself by blaming Beaufort for not consummating their marriage. He had to prove he wasn't impotent before five doctors and a judge of the ecclesiastical court. 'They offered to wait upon his Grace to any *place of public resort* – no, no, he would only go behind the screen, and when he knocked they were to come to him, but come that moment. He was some time behind the scenes: at last he knocked, and the good old folks saw what amazed them – what they had not seen many a day! – [the actor-playwright Colley] Cibber says, "His Grace's prick is in everybody's mouth." He is now upon his mettle and will sue Lord Talbot for fourscore thousand pounds damages.'

The Yale edition of Walpole's *Correspondence*, Vol. 18, p.185

When Oscar went to meet his God,
Not earth to earth but sod to sod,
It was for sinners such as this
Hell was created bottomless.

Prompted by the death of Oscar Wilde and attributed to Swinburne

Post coitum, omne animal triste est.
Someone claimed that this Latin tag – Every animal is sad after
sex – could be matched by the name of the solicitors' firm: Mann,
Rogers & Greaves.

What a strange thing is the propagation of life! A bubble of seed,
which may be spilt in a whore's lap or in the orgasm of a voluptu-
ous dream, might (for aught we know) have formed a Caesar or a
Buonaparte – there is nothing remarkable recorded of their sires
that I know of.

Lord Byron, 'Detached Thoughts', 1821–2

The sexual liberation of adults has been bought at a high price and
it is not the adults who have paid it.

P. D. James

Sea and Shore

... as the crest of some slow-arching wave,
Heard in dead night along that table-shore,
Drops flat, and after the great waters break
Whitening for half a league, and thin themselves
Far over sands marbled with moon and cloud
From less and less to nothing.

Tennyson, 'The Last Tournament', Idylls of the King

... as night-seas on phosphoric bars
Like a flame-plumed fan, shake slowly out their ridgy reach of
   crumbling stars.

Francis Thompson, 'A Judgement of Heaven'

I remember Sam Cox, walking by the seaside as if absorbed in deep
contemplation, was questioned about what he was musing on. He
replied: 'I was wondering that such an almost infinite and unwieldy
element should produce a sprat.'

William Cowper, letter to the Reverend William Unwin, July 1779

Anyone who sleeps within earshot of the sea must be considered
lucky. And Debussy, after all, was sitting in one of Eastbourne's
deck chairs when he first heard the sounds of 'La Mer'.

Penelope Fitzgerald, A House of Air.
She went to boarding-school in Eastbourne.

The retreating water clawing like a croupier at the seething shingle

My Foreign Country: Trevor Fishlock's Britain

Harriet, Lady Granville

'Haryo' was the daughter of Georgiana, Duchess of Devonshire, her husband the long-serving Ambassador to France from the 1820s to the 1840s. Her letters (2 vols, 1894) are full of mordant wit and intelligence, penetrating the pretensions of English and French high society.

Men so little understand the comforts of talking a great deal about nothing at all.

[On her first days as an ambassadress, in Brussels in 1824] I am more convinced than ever that if manners make the man dress makes manners and, strong in the ease of my new corsets, in the tidiness of my new silk gown, feet unentangled in my flounces, and hair crêpé into the solidity of a wig, I behaved to perfection, and returned home with a very comfortable self-approbation and a diminished sense of representation.

I always think it more incumbent on an heiress to be pretty than anyone else, as it leaves a loophole for her admirers and a hope of inspiring for herself a disinterested attachment.

Mr Macaulay dined here [in Paris in 1840] yesterday, and as we had nothing to do but listen he was very welcome. He told us all about everything and is I think prepared for anything.

Some of her devastating thumbnails:
[Mrs Pigot] whom I am convinced if she settled on one would sting

[Mr Drummond] a bore to the bone and large Scotch bones they are

[Mr Beresford] a leach sort of a man, upon whom a title acts as a magnet and who sticks to a ladyship with laudable perseverance

[Miss Parkins] very short and very smart, with a pot of rouge on each cheek

[Count Potocki] Let me introduce you – an immensely fat, good-humoured, gay *garçon*, between forty and fifty, who has no pleasure but in giving it . . . and his fortune being as large as his person, he has the means to do it most splendidly. He is, then, one of those ultra-happy beings who have an utter insensibility to ridicule – a great lesson, it being the only way to disarm it – dances quadrilles *en masse* and in spectacles, acts Cupidon in charades, and laughs louder than those who laugh at him, *ergo* they only laugh with him.

[Lord Clanwilliam] whose zest in society consists in perpetually going too near the wind, and the satisfaction that people in general find in winning the race is found by him in running out of the course

[Lady William Bentinck] a good-natured, kind-hearted, potato-headed woman always in a bother, every second word a blunder

[Mr Edgcombe] very inoffensive. He is not handsome, he is not clever, he is not useful, but there is nothing below mediocre.

[The Russian Ambassador, Fyodor Pahlen] a very handsome fine-looking man . . . Picks his teeth with his knife, scorns sugar tongs, a grand specimen of a Russian soldier.

Scotland

None but those monstrous creatures of God know how to join so much beauty with so much horror. A fig for your poets, painters, gardeners and clergymen that have not been among them. Their imagination can be made up of nothing but bowling greens, flowering shrubs, horse-ponds, Fleet ditches, shell-grottoes and Chinée-rails.

Thomas Gray on the Highlands, 1766

I cannot bear Scotland: in spite of every natural beauty, the people are so odious. Their hospitality takes one in, but that is kept up because it is their pride. Their piety seems to me mere love of argument and prejudice; it is the custom to make a saturnalia of New Year's Eve, and New Year's Day they drown themselves in whisky.

Pamela, Lady Campbell to Emily Eden, 7 January 1821,
Miss Eden's Letters, 1919

He spoke of Hogmanay in the streets of Edinburgh, hot punch and kissing. There used to be gangs of footpads there. C. was once struck on the head by them and had his hat broken. He saw three young men of this kind hanged.

William Allingham, Diary, on a visit to
Thomas Carlyle in Chelsea, 1 January 1873

It is impossible not to esteem them, and they are the best friends – as long as you have fish to fry. If you are doing nothing in particular, they leave you, for they must be getting on . . . To have no particular object in life, but to take it as it comes – you will find this in China, in India, in France, in England; I have not found it in Scotland. I feel as if the country were a company founded to exploit something – if they failed, they would cease to exist.

Walter Raleigh, 1901, Professor of English at Glasgow until 1904

Queen Victoria

Her father, the Duke of Kent, talks to Thomas Creevey in 1817 about his elder brothers and about what is expected of him.
My opinion is the Regent will not attempt a divorce . . . As for the Duke of York, at his time of life and that of the Duchess, all issue, of course, is out of the question. The Duke of Clarence, I have no doubt, will marry if he can; but the terms he asks from the ministers are such as they can never comply with. Besides a settlement such as is proper for a prince who marries expressly for a succession to the throne, the Duke of Clarence demands the payment of all his debts, which are very great, and a handsome provision for each of his ten natural children [by the actress Mrs Jordan]. These are terms which no minister can accede to. Should the Duke of Clarence not marry, the next prince in succession is myself; and though I trust that I shall be at all times ready to obey any call my country may make upon me, God only knows the sacrifice it will be to make, whenever I think it my duty to become a married man. It is now seven and twenty years that Madame St Laurent and I have lived together . . . I shall hope and expect to see justice done by the nation and the ministers to her. She is of very good family and has never been an actress, and I am the first and only person who ever lived with her.
The following year the Duke of Kent married the Princess Victoria of Saxe-Saalfeld-Coburg, who gave birth to the future Queen Victoria in 1819; he died in 1821. George IV (the Regent) did try to divorce Queen Caroline, unsuccessfully, but she also died in 1821. The Duke of Clarence, the future William IV, married Adelaide of Saxe-Meiningen in 1818, but there were no children.

On the day after Victoria had become queen in June 1837:
At twelve she held a Council at which she presided with as much ease as if she had been doing nothing else all her life, and though Lord Lansdowne or Bathurst had contrived between them to make some confusion with the Council papers, she was not put out by

it. She looked very well, and though so small in stature, and without any pretension to beauty, the gracefulness of her manner and
the good expression of her countenance give her on the whole a
very agreeable appearance, and with her youth inspire an excessive
interest in all who approach her, and which I can't help feeling
myself.

Charles Greville, Clerk to the Privy Council, Memoirs

I am a damsel gay and bright
Who like to do the thing that's right,
The secret I don't like to mince,
I have married a buxom German prince.
He brought me sausages so fine,
He kiss'd me well and used me kind,
Thirty thousand pounds he has got a year,
I am married at last and I don't care.

I bought him a dandy shirt so fine,
A pair of boots, and four and nine,
A three cock'd hat and a feather all right,
A great cow heel and a pound of tripe,
I bought him a watch as big as St Paul's,
And a slashing dashing pair of smalls,
I bought him a gun like Oldgate Pump,
And he fired a shot a tiddle le bump.

From a street ballad, 'Married at Last',
composed for Queen Victoria's marriage in 1840

*Albert's annual allowance granted by Parliament was not the expected
£50,000. Four-and-nine is another* double entendre *(see the lyrics of
the Irish song '4 and 9'), while smalls were underpants.*

Dean Hobart of Windsor congratulated the Queen in 1841 on the birth of a son and heir with the consoling thought that she was 'saving us from the incredible curse of a female succession'.

Lord Melbourne said the only time he'd seen Queen Victoria angry was when he said to her, 'But damn it, Madam, you don't expect that he [Albert] will always be faithful to you, do you?' . . . Albert's influence over Victoria gained by degrees – never finished a game of chess with her for the first three years.

Chichester Fortescue, *Diary*, January 1852

Here everything is Scotch – the curtains, the carpets, the furniture are all of different plaids, and the thistles are in such abundance that they would rejoice the heart of a donkey if they happened to look like his favourite repast, which they don't. I am told that it is *de rigueur* to clothe myself in tweed directly . . . It is very cold here, and I believe my feet were frost-bitten at dinner, for there was no fire at all there, and in the drawing-room there were two little sticks which hissed at the man who attempted to light them; and the Queen, thinking, I suppose, that they meant to burn, had a large screen placed between the royal nose and the unignited wood. She seemed, I thought, particularly grateful for such small jokes as my freezing state enabled me to crack. I have a very comfortable room, however, and am now sitting on the hob . . . I must, however, be ready for kirk, where the *meenister* preaches for two hours and takes his large, rough greyhound into the pulpit with him, so no more at present.

Lord Clarendon to his wife, from Balmoral, 1856,
Life and Letters

What you say of the pride of giving life to an immortal soul is very fine, dear, but I own I cannot enter into that; I think much more of our being a cow or a dog in such moments.

Queen Victoria to her daughter Vicky in 1859, shortly before she gave birth to her son, who was to become Kaiser Wilhelm II

Her intense admirer, Lord Beaconsfield [Benjamin Disraeli], himself highly imaginative, once said that if he wanted to forecast the effect of some parliamentary measure on the minds of the middle class, and distrusted his own judgement, he always consulted the Queen and always found he had been right in accepting her opinion . . . She was identical (in this piece of her personality) with the governing class of her subjects, which she saw, long before any of her ministers perceived it, was no longer the aristocracy who then were the landlords of the greater part of English soil, but the middle class.

E. F. Benson, *As We Were,* 1930

The King of Basutoland in southern Africa wrote to Queen Victoria telling her that, 'My Country is your blanket and my people the lice upon it.'

Queen Victoria celebrated her Diamond Jubilee in 1897. When she met him shortly after she asked the Bishop of Winchester, 'From what point did you see the procession?' Then recollecting, she said, 'Oh! You were on the steps of St Paul's. I', she added, 'was unfortunate – I had a very bad place and saw nothing.'

When Queen Victoria died in 1901, her grandson Kaiser Wilhelm II measured her for her coffin and the London prostitutes wore mourning.

Death

> Successive nights like rolling waves
> Convey them quickly, who are bound for Death.
>
> George Herbert, 'Mortification'

Mozart said in one of his letters that he thought of death each day, and that this was the wellspring of his music.

Lord Guilford died of an inflammation of the bowels: so they took them out, and sent them (on account of their discrepancies), separately from the carcass, to England. Conceive a man going one way, and his intestines another, and his immortal soul a third! – Was there ever such a distribution? One certainly has a soul; but how it came to allow itself to be enclosed in a body is more than I can imagine. I only know if once mine gets out, I'll have a bit of a tussle before I get it in again to that or any other.

Lord Byron to Thomas Moore, from Venice, 1817

Why attack God? He may be as unhappy as we are.

Eric Satie to his atheist friends, on his deathbed

The anonymous telegram meant to have been sent to Jacques Maritain shortly after André Gide's death: *L'enfer n'existe pas. Avertissez Claudel. Amusez-vous. Gide.* Maritain was a distinguished Catholic academic and Claudel a Catholic playwright.

Ramon Maris Narvaez, three times president of government in Spain in the 1850s–60s, asked on his deathbed to forgive his enemies, replied, 'I have none. I have had them all shot.'

Sir Thomas Bradford, Commander-in-Chief Bombay, and his wife were sailing home in 1829 when she died at St Helena.
Her devoted husband preserved her body in spirits, and, not properly watching the cask, it was tapped by the sailors, many of whom died from the effects of the poison.

Elizabeth Grant, Memoirs of a Highland Lady

William Dalrymple in his travel book *In Xanadu* tells a similar story about his three-times great-grandfather James Pattle. He died in India and his widow put him in a cask of rum for the voyage home. It exploded one night and this sent her immediately off her head. She then died, raving. The cask was nailed down again and put on board ship but the sailors bored a hole in it and got drunk on the rum. The ship caught fire, hit a rock and blew up.

We are journeying towards the Grand Silence; what lies beyond it earthly man has never known, nor will know: but all brave men have known that it was Godlike, that it was right Good – that the name of it was God . . . Tho' He slay me yet will I trust him. '*Eterno amore*'; that is the ultimate significance of this wild clashing whirlwind which is named Life, where the sons of Adam flicker painfully for an hour.

Thomas Carlyle to the dying John Stirling, 1844

In the seventeenth century one would have been more likely to have buried someone younger rather than older than oneself. In 1790 recorded baptisms exceeded recorded deaths in London for the first time, a key moment in the decline of the death rate in Britain. It was only in the 1920s that medicine started to cure more than it killed. There are more people alive today than have died since the world began.

Sleep sweetly, tender heart, in peace:
Sleep, holy spirit, blessed soul,
While the stars burn, the moons increase,
And the great ages onward roll.

Sleep till the end, true soul and sweet.
Nothing comes to thee new or strange.
Sleep full of rest from head to feet;
Lie still, dry dust, secure of change.

Tennyson, 'To T. S.', Elegy on Edward Spedding

King: Now, Hamlet, where's Polonius?

Hamlet: At supper.

King: At supper! Where?

Hamlet: Not where he eats, but where he is eaten: a certain convocation of politic worms are e'en at him. Your worm is your only emperor for diet: we fat all creatures else to fat us, and we fat ourselves for maggots: your fat king and your fat beggar is but variable service, two dishes but to one table: that's the end.

King: Alas! Alas!

Hamlet: A man may fish with the worm that hath eat of a king, and eat the flesh that have fed of that worm.

King: What dost thou mean by this?

Hamlet: Nothing, but to show how a king may go a progress through the guts of a beggar.

Hamlet of course has killed Polonius. Anthony Daniels quoted this exchange in an essay he wrote about meeting a distinguished forensic entomologist. It comes in Act III. In the famous gravedigger's scene in Act V, Hamlet returns to this sort of conceit when he asks, 'Why may not imagination trace the noble dust of Alexander till he find it stopping a bunghole?'

Mr Palmer Robinson, going with Lord Pomfret in a hackney coach to Hyde Park to fight a duel, just as they turned into the Park they met an empty hearse, upon which Robinson thrusts his head out of the window and calls out with great generosity, 'Here, you fellow with the hell cart, if you'll stay a minute or two, I'll give you a fare.'

The 2nd Viscount Palmerston, d. 1802,
from *Portrait of a Whig Peer,* ed. Brian Connell, 1957

The long habit of living indisposeth us for dying.

Sir Thomas Browne, *Urn Burial*

In 1789 London was convulsed by the murder of Lord Sandwich's mistress outside Covent Garden Opera House. The murderer, a clergyman infatuated with her, had two pistols and there was an argument as to why between Dr Johnson and Topham Beauclerk, whose contribution concerned a Mr Delmis –
who loved buttered muffins, but durst not eat them because they disagreed with his stomach, [so] resolved to shoot himself; and then he ate three buttered muffins for breakfast, before shooting himself, knowing that he should not be troubled with indigestion; *he* had two charged pistols.

Boswell, *Life of Johnson*

Some causes of death in the twentieth century: 20 million in the First World War; between 50 and 100 million from Spanish influenza in 1918–19 (wherever it came from, it wasn't Spain); 17 million victims of Nazism; 100 million victims of Communism.

O eloquent, just and mighty Death! Whom none could advise, thou has persuaded.

Sir Walter Raleigh, *History of the World,* 1614

Mixed Motives and Self-Deception

It is not in the nature of men to act ideally, and we know today that the nearest we can get, any of us, to sincerity is perhaps a genuine self-deception.

C. V. Wedgwood, *History and Hope*, 1987

Life is the art of being well deceived; and in order that the deception may succeed, it must be habitual and uninterrupted. A constant examination of the value of our opinions and enjoyments, compared with those of others, may lessen our prejudices, but will leave nothing for our affections to rest upon.

William Hazlitt, 'On Pedantry', *The Round Table*, 1817

[The Miss Bertrams'] vanity was in such good order, that they seemed to be quite free from it, and gave themselves no airs; while the praises attending such behaviour, secured and brought round by their aunt [Mrs Norris], served to strengthen them in believing they had no faults.

Jane Austen, *Mansfield Park*

As we walked along the Strand tonight, arm in arm, a woman of the town accosted us, in the usual enticing manner. 'No, no, my girl,' said Johnson, 'it won't do.' He, however, did not treat her with harshness, and we talked of the wretched life of such women, and agreed, that much more misery than happiness, upon the whole, is produced by illicit commerce between the sexes. [Four nights later Boswell picked up a prostitute, arguing this time that 'Surely . . . when the woman is already abandoned, the crime must be alleviated.']

James Boswell, *Life of Johnson*

Men little think how immorally they act in rashly meddling with what they do not understand. Their delusive good intention is no sort of excuse for their presumption. They who truly mean well must be fearful of acting ill.

Edmund Burke, *Appeal from the New to the Old Whigs*, 1791

The novelist Barbara Pym wrote somewhere of the common desire to do good without much personal inconvenience.

[Mr Bulstrode] was doctrinally convinced that there was a total absence of merit in himself; but that doctrinal conviction may be held without pain when the sense of demerit does not take a distinct shape in memory and revive the tingling of shame or the pang of remorse. Nay, it may be held with intense satisfaction, when the depth of our sinning is but a measure for the depth of forgiveness, and clenching proof that we are peculiar instruments of the divine intention . . .

George Eliot, *Middlemarch*

We mortals always try and trace a consistency in character which is an ingredient never to be found in any composition, foreign to human nature altogether, which we still hunt after, and refer to and talk of, as if it was not as ideal as the philosopher's stone, a tortoise-shell tom cat, or any other impossibility.

Pamela, Lady Campbell, *Miss Eden's Letters*

Acknowledgements

The author and publisher would like to thank the following for permission to reproduce copyright material: p. 14, Nicholas Cooper; p. 15, Simon Jenkins, Jonathan Meades; pp. 19 and 65, Professor Deirdre McCloskey; p. 21, Simon Winder; p. 22, the estate of Keith Vaughan, c/o DACS; p. 25, Professor Dick Davies; pp. 25 and 98, passages by Penelope Fitzgerald, HarperCollins Publishers; pp. 17, 34 and 98, Trevor Fishlock; p. 30, Anthony Powell, David Higham literary agents; pp. 34 and 97, Matt Ridley; p. 36, Jonathan Meades; p. 38, Jonathan Sumption, Charles Moore; p. 39, by permission of the Isaiah Berlin Literary Trust; p. 47, P. J. Kavanagh, Carcanet Press; p. 50, Nicholas Hodgson; p. 51, Peter Parker and Isabel Colegate; p. 53, J. H. Plumb, Springer Nature BV (Palgrave Scholarly); p. 56, Sir Nicholas Braithwaite in *Parting Shots*, Penguin 2010, used under the Open Government Licence; p. 76, Raymond Asquith, John Jolliffe.

Every effort has been made to trace the holders of copyright material but in the event that we have failed to do so we would be pleased to hear from them. Please contact Slightly Foxed, 53 Hoxton Square, London NI 6PB.